DISCARDED

The Teaching for Social Justice Series

William Ayers—Series Editor
Therese Quinn—Associate Series Editor

Editorial Board: Hal Adams, Barbara Bowman, Lisa Delpit, Michelle Fine, Maxine Greene, Caroline Heller, Annette Henry, Asa Hilliard, Rashid Khalidi, Gloria Ladson-Billings, Charles Payne, Mark Perry, Luis Rodriguez, Jonathan Silin, William Watkins

Writing in the Asylum

Student Poets in City Schools

JENNIFER McCORMICK
Foreword by Michelle Fine

Teachers College, Columbia University
New York and London

"Abandoned Church" from *Poet in New York* by Federico Garcia Lorca. Translation copyright © 1988 by The Estate of Federico Garcia Lorca, and Greg Simon and Steven F. White. Reprinted by permission of Farrar, Straus and Giroux, LLC.

"Eulogy for Alvin Frost", from *The Black Unicorn* by Audre Lorde. Copyright © 1978 by Audre Lorde. Used by permission of W.W. Norton & Company, Inc.

Sections of Chapter 4 appeared in McCormick, J., "Drag Me to the Asylum: Disguising and Asserting Identities in Urban Schools," *The Urban Review, 35*(2), June 2003. Used by permission of Kluwer Academic/Plenum Publishers.

Lines from "Ars Poetica": "The purpose of poetry . . . guests come in and out at will." From *The Collected Poems 1931-1987* by Czeslaw Milosz. Copyright © 1988 by Czeslaw Milosz Royalties, Inc. Reprinted by permission of HarperCollins Publishers Inc.

Morisseau-Leroy, Felix. Tonton Makout. *Callaloo* 15:3 (1992), 673-674. © Charles H. Rowell. Reprinted with permission of The John Hopkins University Press.

Moss, Thylias. Holding. *Callaloo* 16:1 (1993), 18-19. © Charles H. Rowell. Reprinted with permission of The Johns Hopkins University Press.

Published by Teachers College Press, 1234 Amsterdam Avenue, New York, NY 10027

Library of Congress Cataloging-in-Publication Data

McCormick, Jennifer.
    Writing in the asylum : student poets in city schools / Jennifer McCormick;
  foreword by Michelle Fine
    p. cm. — (The teaching for social justice series)
  Includes bibliographical references (p.) and index
  ISBN 0-8077-4490-5 (cloth : alk. paper) — ISBN 0-8077-4489-1 (pbk.: alk. paper)
    1. High school student's writings, American—New York (State)—New York—History and criticism. 2. School verse, American—New York (State)—New York—History and criticism. 3. American poetry—New York (State)—New York—History and criticism. 4. English language—Composition and exercises—Study and teaching (Secondary)— New York (State)—New York. 5. Poetry—Authorship—Study and teaching (Secondary)—New York (State)—New York. 6. Creative writing (Secondary education)—New York (State)—New York. 7. High school students—New York (State)— New York—Intellectual life. 8. New York (N.Y.)—Intellectual life. 9. New York (N.Y.)—In literature. I. Title
  PS255.N5M36 2004
  811'.54099283'097471—dc22   2004048032

ISBN 0-8077-4489-1 (paper)
ISBN 0-8077-4490-5 (cloth)

Printed on acid-free paper
Manufactured in the United States of America

11   10   09   08   07   06   05   04   8   7   6   5   4   3   2   1

To Nikki Richardson,
Nessa Myers,
Jhoy Meade, and
Tanzania Roach,
with love and gratitude.

Contents

Foreword

It's been 50 years since Brown v. the Board of Education, and still, from within the tomb-like structures of urban comprehensive high schools, African American and Latino youth are more likely to disappear than graduate. Betrayed by the cumulative consequences of finance inequity and persistent racism, commodified by the prison industrial complex, and deceived by neoliberal federal and state policy that promises accountability and assures abandonment, it comes as no surprise that drop-out rates are spiking across the nation, particularly for students of color. The consequences are more severe than ever. Over 70% of women and men in prison have neither a GED nor a high school diploma. In New York State, it is estimated that 80% of prisoners come from seven districts in New York City—seven comprehensive high school zones. The hollowing of public education for the vast majority of urban youth of color can no longer be theorized or researched in isolation from the swelling of the mass incarceration system (Fine & Torre, in press). *Writing in the Asylum: Student Poets in City Schools* leads our twin analyses of public education within a political context of surveillance and mass incarceration for communities of color.

Wandering through the catacombs like a tour guide, Jennifer McCormick eavesdrops on the echoes of poetry produced despite/because of/at the core of the "asylum." Whispers of outrage, pain, and revolution thread with waves of laughter, wisdom, and generosity. Within the very same walls we feel the vibrations of scanners, the invasion of metal detectors, the deadening drip feed of miseducation that Carter Woodson (1992) loathed so long ago and the jazzy rhythm of young women's spoken word. In these spaces, promises are broken and spirits are, too. Bodies are violated and imaginations soar. Herein lies the paradoxical public institution of schooling to which McCormick, joined by committed educators and talented young poets, reveals the resilience and wisdom that sing through the fog.

The contemporary urban comprehensive high school, as in the past, fills with ghosts (Fine, 1991; Gordon, 1996). When first we enter UHS, we meet adults and youth, in the line up, "waiting" to "go" to school. While on line I wondered, "With this welcoming scene at front door, what does it mean to 'go' to school? For what are these young people 'waiting'?" With McCormick as our guide, we pass through the metal detectors and turn the corner to witness educators midwifing the future, working to help students birth their spoken and written words. At this intellectual, cultural, and emotional intersection of state, body, and voice, stuffed into a tiny hole in a building so thoroughly lacking, "tongues of fire" electrify. Illuminating what is, these young poets dare to speak for what could be (Anzaldua, 1999; Greene, 1995).

Among the finest of contemporary young ethnographers of urban schooling, Jennifer McCormick has given us an understanding of the raw contradictions that constitute public schooling for urban youth. Borrowing from Foucault and Freire, hooks and Lorde, she traces educational policy and practice as they redline those long-forgotten neighborhoods of poverty and color in urban America. Refusing the theoretical binaries of reproduction and resistance, panopticon and possibility, McCormick paints an institution deprived of oxygen, where young women breathe fire. She allows us to visit the corners of the "asylum" in which spirits soar, dreams flourish, words fly on a wing. Theoretically, she challenges determinism with poetry and she insists that humanism be tamed with biting class, race, and gender analyses.

No stranger to critical theory, Jennifer McCormick theorizes schools as contested spaces in which material deprivation weighs heavily, while lights of hope flicker. She understands and narrates the complex dialectics of oppression as she invites readers to feel the spasms of a larynx yearning to speak. She assails public institutions that penetrate young bodies of color with suspicion and surveillance, and she encourages young poets in their desire to voice, to feel, to rebel, to be known, and to be heard. She hides none of her disdain for an educational institution that has trampled the dreams of the young, and she pays her due respect to those educators who persist, smuggling in just a bit of space for youth to be educated.

The structure of *Writing in the Asylum* brilliantly embodies McCormick's complex theoretical framing. By alternating her analytic gaze between violations and poetry, McCormick allows us to see how educational policy and practice can smother body and soul and, at the same time, provoke mind and spirit. Through her ethnographic craft, we witness the transformative power of the arts and the cumulative devastation wrought by the "soul murder" of the urban comprehensive high school (Painter, 1998). With cynical ambivalence about institutions and uncompromised belief in youth, Jennifer McCormick demands that we hear that in the asylum, desire, yearning, and passion swim in the same stream with pain, outrage, and despair; even in high school, even in one of the poorest neighborhoods in America, even as we drown in neo-liberal policies that erode the dream.

This book marks a significant turn within critical educational studies. McCormick refuses to tell a simple story of poetry, and with equal force, she resists telling a simple story of oppression. *Writing in the Asylum* tells two stories at once: the struggle for a public sphere of educational possibility and the struggle for the souls of poor and working-class young women of color from whom America has walked away. Although McCormick worries that she will conflate "student individuality and structural inequities," she successfully insists that readers bear witness to their intimate alliance.

Like so many who write about aesthetic wisdom borne in the ashes of injustice—only much better—McCormick asks readers, and the state, to confront the choices we have made/are making 50 years after Brown, in the dawn of the 21st century. Holding a mirror to our collective shame, Jennifer McCormick, the educators, and the young women with whom she writes, remind us that we can, right now, by doing nothing, choose to pour the final bucket of cement onto carceral schooling, securing its place in the foundation of urban America. Or we can invest in the wisdom, intelligence, and poetry of poor and working-class youth of color, waiting only to be watered.

—Michelle Fine
The Graduate Center, CUNY

REFERENCES

Anzaldua, G. (1999). *Borderlands/La frontera*. San Francisco: Aunt Lute Publishers.

Fine, M. (1991). *Framing dropouts: Notes on the politics of an urban public high school*. Albany: State University of New York Press.

Fine, M., & Torre, M. (in press). Re-membering exclusions: Participatory action research within public institutions. *Qualitative Studies in Psychology*.

Gordon, A. (1996). *Ghostly matters*. Minneapolis: University of Minnesota Press.

Greene, M. (1995). *Releasing the imagination: Essays on education, the arts, and social change*. San Francisco: Jossey-Bass.

Painter, N. I. (1998). *Soul murder and slavery*. Baylor, TX: Baylor University Press.

Woodson, C. (1992). *The miseducation of the Negro*. New York: Communication Systems.

Acknowledgments

Many people have lived with this book and live through its pages. Richard Blot, John Devine, Michelle Fine, Peter Lucas, and Gordon Pradl supported my research interest in urban schooling and hence helped launch the initial stages of this project. My deepest thanks to: Patricia Calderwood, Geri Deluca, Marylou Gramm, Nancy Hoch, Julia Kasdorf, Roberta Satow, and Peter Taubman, who repeatedly read drafts of the manuscript and whose ideas have strengthened the final text.

Two grants sponsored by the City University of New York allowed me to complete the manuscript. I want to thank Nora Eisenberg for having the foresight to establish the Faculty Publication Program at the City University of New York. A Brooklyn College grant provided me with funds and time to write. I am indebted to John Devine for launching and directing the School Partnership Program at New York University. I would like to thank my editors, Catherine Bernard, Catherine Chandler, and Carole Saltz for critical insight. William Ayers and Therese Quinn saw a book long before there was one. Countless people who live and work in New York City have inspired me with extraordinary displays of energy; space allows mention of only a few: to David Fletcher for single-handedly wiring the Bronx, your commitment to equity and access is exceptional; to Nancy Shapiro, for your generosity and willingness to direct the Teachers and Writers Collaborative, a place where both poetry and teenagers thrive. Numerous students allowed me to cite their poetry years after sitting in Hermine Meinhard's workshops. Special thanks to Gerald Dussap, Lakee Farley, Kenneth Francis, Shakeya Flenory, Andre Isaacs, Kashan Larry, Nadia McGrouder, and Tsahay Matthias. I only hope my work honors your trust. My family was supportive in multiple and often invisible ways; to my husband, Cesar Ayala, for balancing work and pleasure; to my son, Diego Ayala McCormick, for bringing me much joy and giving me yet another reason to struggle for an academically rigorous *public* school system; to my parents William and Marguerite McCormick, political activists who fight, and taught me to fight, for a socially just society. Finally, I am profoundly indebted to Hermine Meinhard, whose artistry and teaching have been, and undoubtedly will continue to be, a source of inspiration.

Writing in the Asylum

Student Poets in City Schools

Introduction

I am luna
I would rather be the moon than the sun
If I were the moon
I'd show just how much of me
I'd want everyone to see
—Tanzania, age 17

Tanzania, or "Tanzie," as she calls herself, wrote "I Am Luna" while sitting in a classroom. She read a definition of metaphor on the chalkboard in her English class and then wrote the poem.

Like Tanzania, the students at Urban High School (UHS), a comprehensive, segregated high school in Brooklyn, wrote often. Kerryann copied songs and stories from Jamaica onto loose-leaf paper. Jhoy typed up 20 poems, stapled them, and distributed the book to her tutors. Other young men and women filled notebooks with rap, imitating the structure honed by published artists. In a school now slated for closure, poetry was everywhere: in notebooks, on walls, and on loose sheets of paper. Overwhelmed by its ubiquity, I collected it. Its meaning has since become the subject of this book.

After the attacks on the World Trade Center, my New York City neighborhood was awash in photographs of the dead and poetry. At first, a few lines appeared on walls, and words were printed out of dust on car windshields. But after a few days the city was covered in paper—long missives, rhymes, abstractions—so much so that one fire chief pleaded, "Please, no more poetry." Poetry became synonymous with both grief and perseverance. Its hold on the public's imagination, its ubiquity, has convinced me that poetry is necessary for children who believe that "if I go to this school, I must be worth nothing." As William Burroughs once said, "All warm-blooded animals have to dream. If they can't dream, they die. It's a logical extension to suppose that without art, people can't exist" (as cited in Damon 1993, p. 100). I have come to see the poems written at UHS as emotional preserves, "sanctuaries for dreams and frightening ideas" (Lorde, 1984, p. 39), within structures too often defined by dehumanization.

BACKGROUND

> JENNIFER: You said that when you're scanned you feel out of your
> element. What does that mean?
> TANZANIA: I feel like they are trying to get to know my body.

During the 1992–1993 school year, I worked alongside a poet in this Brooklyn high school and began to look at how poetry offered students a way to transcend physical and psychological containment. Specifically, I became interested in how the associational leaps of *lyric* poetry allowed teenagers to distance themselves from criminal categories and express vulnerability, fear, joy, and anger—emotions not easily conveyed in a school patrolled by 17 uniformed guards and one New York City police officer. *Writing in the Asylum* thus has contradictory meanings: asylum is a Goffmanesque institution that strips the individual of her identity, and yet it is also her sanctuary.

The students at UHS asserted their individuality and disguised themselves through multiple venues (dress and visual art come to mind), but poetry was one of the more complex mediums open to them. It allowed flexibility: the expression of tangible reality, repressed selves, and unconscious knowledge. Poetry replicated the constraints of time and place and reflected a kind of freedom from both. Student work often emerged from the interplay between personal psychic reality and control (over language and self-presentation). Through masks, metaphor, and nonrational associations, they accessed the unconscious and explored emotions that were below the surface of daily perception. Their work was often the battleground between the conscious and the unconscious life. Two years after she wrote "I Am Luna," Tanzania told me: "[Poems] are harder to write than stories. You can't ramble in a poem. You have to get somewhere quickly. I write to get feeling out. My poems don't have story—I want the feeling. I'm not giving the story. I'm giving you anger." Such emotional intensity seemed to emerge from a kind of mental focus, which liberated students from temporal and spatial constraints. In his definition of the lyric, Northrop Frye (1985) focuses on a turning away from narration or sequential experience: "The superimposing [that comes when one sheds "real time"] provides an intense concentration of emotion and imagery" (p. 33).

Writing was thus akin to dreaming: It allowed the writer to reinvent how the sensory world feels. Poet and essayist Wayne Dodd (1992) claims that reinvention, in dreams and in poetry, hinges on feeling. "How the phenomenal world feels to me, as it is made available to my senses, is what makes it seem true, makes it feel actual, continuing" (p. 120). If poetry allows a rein-vention of our sensory world, if it makes the phenomenal world feel real, it provides a way out of our waking lives—and an escape from containment. Teens wrote lyric, or transcendent, poetry from thought processes that were not necessarily linear. Their use of persona and imagery, and their willingness to connect wildly dissimilar objects opened a space for the unconscious, and in that space they described children who eat their mother's body, they con-jured the dead, and they became women who revealed themselves at will.

Transcendence accompanied conscious efforts to preserve relationships and to bemoan daily experience—by acknowledging what one woman called "the everyday holes in my sneakers." In addition to the lyric, students com-posed prosaic, sometimes journalistic, pieces out of material reality. They wrote what they saw; what they heard. They wrote whatever fit into their lives. Poetry became a vehicle of self-narration. By taking daily observations and writing a poem, they transformed their experiences into an aesthetic whole. The transformation required a kind of suppleness that enabled them to perceive an event from multiple perspectives. In Chapter 2, for example, writing the circumstances of one's life prompted one 16-year-old to confront and take solace in her self and her surroundings. Through dialogue, the author holds together and synthesizes two conflicting perceptions of self—she is both orphaned child and mother. She imagines and garners strength from the mother/caretaker's voice, and ultimately sees what may not have been seen: "I am strong and I will put this behind me." For this writer, inter-nal dialogue becomes an asylum, and by writing it she saves her will, her strength, and her self-complexity.

Alongside my students' poetry and their nuanced portrayals of self, school, and neighborhood, I forge one of the main arguments of the book: namely, that a desire to protect students and teachers has nearly destroyed traditional conceptions of school, allowing state and city bureaucracies to graft new measures of assessment, new norms, and a new, far more repressive architecture over early 20th-century buildings. UHS does not resemble the factory-like institutions that assessed and promoted an earlier generation of immigrants. The look and feel of the school—its continual use of locked doors, barbed wire, hand-held metal detectors, and uniformed guards—invokes thoughts of a prison complex. We see, in its security apparatus, a fun-damental opposition to earlier notions of schooling when administrators "crammed as much learning as possible into [a single] day, intensifying the use of movement" (Bracken, 1992, p. 234). Efficiency, once modeled by fac-tory-line production, has broken down. Time often stood still at UHS, as students waited to be searched for weapons, as they waited to insert ID cards into a tracking machine. Academic assessment, moreover, was frequently rendered meaningless.

Schooling practices, like scanning (a routine that requires students to assume a criminal stance, with hands out and legs spread) generate the sense, if not the actuality, of social quarantine. However well-intentioned, the use of metal detectors (or scanners), x-ray machines, and uniformed security guards mimic the police surveillance prevalent in Black and Latino neighborhoods. According to Tanzania, "The outside has been brought in. Racial profiling has been brought in; someone in a group is dangerous, so everyone becomes suspect." Ironically, the *inside* has also moved *out*. Corporate officials at Discovery Zone, an indoor playground for toddlers, hired security guards and installed metal detectors in areas where the New York City Board of Education scans students for weapons. Consequently, these pay-to-play stores have walk-through metal detectors in every borough, except Staten Island (which is largely White and working class) (Sacher, 1995, p. A3).

Reflexivity aside, Tanzie's statement—the outside has been brought in—raises haunting questions about the relationship between schooling and social trends. The metal detectors, barbed wire, and steel locks prevalent in city schools remind us that African Americans from New York City to Los Angeles have been imprisoned at an alarming rate. In 1995, the year many of my students graduated, just under one-third of African American men in their 20s were incarcerated, on parole, or on probation (Gest, 1995). Sociologists Becky Pettit and Bruce Western (2004) argue that the incarceration rate for Black men who have dropped out of high school is so pervasive that it constitutes a life course event. Although crime rates explain 80% of the trend, "a significant residual suggests that Blacks are punitively policed, prosecuted, and sentenced" (p. 4). It is chilling to think that punitive policing and survellience may actually begin to occur in the 9th grade.

By acknowledging and condemning the security apparatus in UHS, I am not suggesting that violence did not exist. During the 1980s the school's reputation as a violent place solidified, with reason. Six intruders once entered the classroom of a Jamaican teacher, approached him, put a gun to his head in front of an entire class, and pulled the trigger twice. The gun was empty and the boys ran away, but the teacher was so shaken, he was unable to return to school (Devine, 1990, p. 169). The random nature of violence horrified people who lived and worked in the area. Mothers kept their children inside locked apartments. Teachers feared their own students. Teens sought safety transfers, or dropped out. One woman told me: "My nephew was a nervous wreck. He never finished high school."

Violence existed at UHS, but I argue that the political response to violence and the subsequent restructuring of urban schools has been racialized. After two white teens murdered 11 people at Columbine High School, school violence became a national problem. Politicians and media commentators looked at frightened teenagers jumping out of classroom windows and asked, "What went wrong?" In an editorial for the *New York Times*, entitled "When They Are Us," Orlando Patterson described the nation's shock, noting that: "Nearly all the commentaries about the massacre in Colorado seem to share the assumption that the behavior of the killers reflects some deep failure in the nation's culture—in our treatment of violence and in the way we bring up our children." He contextualizes this shock, saying that the killers' race and class were never the focus of discussion: "If the terrorist act of White, middle-class teen-agers creates an orgy of national soul-searching, then surely the next time a heinous crime is committed by underclass Latino kids, we should engage in the same kind of national self-examination" (Patterson, 1999, p. A31). In March 1992, a week after a Black teenager shot and killed two students at Thomas Jefferson High School in Brooklyn, Chancellor Joseph Fernandez ordered the installation of electromagnetic doors and metal detectors in 41 New York City Schools (Dillon, 1993b, p. 1). Fernandez's reaction was an example of a school system's attempt to contain students and curtail violence. National self-examination never accompanied the ensuing use of high-tech security.

Nikki, Tanzania, Nessa, and Jhoy, along with select teens (young men as well as women), whose writing appears in this book, controlled self-representation, probed experience, and elided simplistic classifications by writing poetry. The content of their work challenges unilateral perceptions of Black teenagers. In conversation with them, I have attempted to convey the complex realities of a city school. This book, like their poetry, registers efforts to escape containment.

Throughout the book, I attempt to strike a balance between ethnography and theoretical analysis. In Chapters 2 and 3, I implicitly link the presence of metal detectors at UHS to architectural designs that bunker African American and Black immigrant populations in central Brooklyn. If taken metaphorically, metal scanners not only symbolize institutional power and individual degradation, but also economic quarantine. They represent the widening disparity of wealth along racial lines in urban centers, the effects of hypersegregation (capital flight and declining city services), and the absence of academically rigorous public schools in Black neighborhoods. I am aware that by wielding a metaphor anchored in images of containment, I run the risk of conflating student individuality and structural inequality. Ethnographic work, the citation of poetry, and unstructured interviews highlight the concrete manifestations of late 20th-century racism on individual teenagers, and it conveys a response to that racism.

In concrete terms, individual works, or words, reveal *both* the "everyday holes in my sneakers" and the willingness "to get behind your troubles." By writing, Nikki, Tanzie, Nessa, and Jhoy learned to attend to non-rational experiences—to the feelings in their emotional lives. Their work conveyed a complexity, a particularity; it became some of my most compelling data.

POETRY IS NOT A LUXURY

Writing to cross psychological boundaries, to preserve social connections, to express fear, and to escape the constraints imposed by time and place are themes woven through this book. However, the book's structure highlights two major distinctions in the poets' written work. In Chapters 2 and 3, poetry interfaces with the writers' immediate surroundings. Students wrote against the marginalization of their neighborhood, and thus they wrote against the concept of throw-away society. The criminalization of a Black population extended into UHS, becoming visible in the school's security practices. Paradoxically, the school criminalized its students in order to protect them. This paradox was never directly replicated in the poetry, but it rested alongside an unsettling parallel: teens often denied the interactive selves that articulated their work. This unwillingness or inability to see themselves as actively creative must have been reinforced in a school where they were perceived as both students and suspects. As suspects, they had to deny the conceptions of themselves brought from home and from childhood. The repercussions of such self-denial were never compartmentalized; they emerged from time to time in student poetry. Despite abnegation, young people wrote proactively to assert control over social circumstances and to move beyond physical and temporal constraints.

In Chapter 4, poetry moves beyond social surroundings—illuminating how the writer is of the world but not in it. Here students re-see the realities of everyday life with renewed clarity. This kind of writing echoes Freud's perception of dreams: "The unsophisticated waking judgment of someone who has just woken from sleep assumes that his dreams, even if they did not come from another world, had at all events carried him off into another world" (1900/1998, p. 42). Released from the usual ways of thinking, released from the constraints of linear writing, poets envisioned a different way of feeling.

Adrienne Rich has weighed the possibility that poetry is powerless, "that it can have nothing to do with the powers that organize us as a society, as communities within that society, as relationships within communities" (Rich, 1993, p. xiv). Yet its potential power haunts her. And in a book that documents the relative isolation of American poets, she writes: "In a society where every public decision has to be justified in the scales of corporate profits, poetry unsettles these apparently self-evident propositions—not through ideology, but by its very presence and ways of being, its embodiment of states of longing and desire"(p. xv). These states of longing are evident in the poetry cited in this text; they replace external perceptions with lines and lives that are hard to pin down.

After graduating, Nessa, a UHS student, worked as a laundry attendant and as a cashier in a 99-cent store. On the eve of the millennium, we talked about our plans for the new year and she quietly asked, "How many days do you work?" "Four," I said, "and you?" "I work eight hours a day, six, sometimes seven days a week." Writing poetry rarely, if ever, led to a living wage, but it developed and nurtured a self-confidence that allowed teenagers to become the center of social interaction. Three years after she took her first writing workshop, Nessa said, "I still write. Friends ask me to write for them. I know I have the talent."

And there is Tanzania, another young woman who sat in poetry workshops at UHS, then returned to her former junior high school to teach poetry. In doing so, she taught others to control self-representation through language:

> I did an exercise . . . something you told me to do. I told the class
> to tell me what they felt, what they saw. One girl, DeMille, known
> as a bad, crazy girl, wrote about Trinidad. She put herself right
> there. She told me how the sun felt on her skin. She described the
> color of her drink. I was so proud. That's when I knew they could
> do it. Toward the end of the month, we had a party. We had just
> finished sewing Japanese books. DeMille didn't show up but came
> late and we talked for a long time. She was so happy that I was
> proud of her—that she was no longer the crazy, bad girl. She could
> write, and speak to me.

Poetry will not alleviate the tedium that accompanies a minimum-wage job or the structural failures that have plagued New York City's public school system, but it provided space for lament, fantasy, and elation, and may have given teens a reason to show up at school doors. As Nessa once said, "Poetry gave me stability. It took away the pain. I think it kept me in school." As she spoke I remember thinking that writing and survival were synonymous.

CHAPTER 1

She Gave Me a Poet's Name

This is who I am
I sit here and talk
to myself.
As you yell I sit and
yell back not with words
but with feelings.
—Nikki, age 15

MEMORIES OF A SCHOOL

Before I ever entered Urban High School to tutor students, I had memories of it. The school sits directly across the street from a state school for the deaf where I had taught from 1986 to 1988, so I had watched the high school for quite some time—its stone structure, its barbed wire fences, its students. Once during a public ceremony at the school for the deaf, UHS teens watched from across the street, tracing signs with their hands, attempting to follow. In another memory, a boy is running to his teacher, pointing in the direction of UHS and signing "blood" and "cop," repeatedly. His eyes are wide with excitement. This last image fixes the perception of much of the school's staff. Many of the teachers at the school for the deaf fear the Urban High School students who "stand outside all day." They fear the lone teens hidden inside hooded sweatshirts. They fear Black teens, city teens. They drive quickly into the school parking lot in the morning, and go home to segregated White neighborhoods at night. Once inside the school building, they, we, remain there, repeating stories about past muggings and watching police vans from across a narrow street. In the fall of 1988, on the first day of school, a teenager is shot on the stairs of the high school for his leather jacket. He dies 2 days after school reopens for another academic year.

Three years later, I began tutoring at Urban High School, in a collaborative program between New York University's Center for Urban Education and New York City's Board of Education. Haunted by the shooting, I tried, in vain, to be reassigned to a "safer" neighborhood. When the appointment was final, I looked for reassurances, yet received few. A day before six graduate students and I entered the school, one of the program directors warned: "Inform your team coordinator of your whereabouts at all times. Stay together, travel together. Two years ago, a student was shot on the steps of UHS."

Memories of my first day at UHS are fragmented and could be images of any large comprehensive high school. Windows line the length of one classroom. Light streams in and highlights painted walls faded to a non-descript pastel. Paint has peeled off an area of the room, leaving stretches of white plaster. A poster, worn and discolored, announces, "You can do anything."

Outside the room, a girl chases a boy down an empty hall. He smiles broadly. Two Haitian girls, dressed in pink ruffled dresses, sit in the cafeteria. Their clothing reminds me of a child's expectations; it is a flutter of girlhood. I imagine they have dressed for what they, or their parents, or their grandparents, think is school. Now they sit, seemingly stunned, barely making eye contact with the adults who question them. One eventually smiles when an NYU graduate student speaks to her in French. On the blackboard directly inside the small, cluttered tutoring room, someone has scrawled, "I will be back." The letters are large, unsteady, child-like.

Urban High School was a deeply contradictory place. Metal detectors, locked doors, and New York City police officers were present alongside girls in pink dresses and teachers with detailed lesson plans. My notes, taken over a 3-year period, are replete with descriptions of a school prepared for potential violence, and classrooms marked by an easy, social spontaneity:

> Entering the building, I take a close look at the scanners, machines used to detect weapons. Two sit opposite each other at a side entrance to the school. They lay dormant—resembling the devices used at an airport. I then proceed up to the fifth floor of the high school to observe a human services elective—a course currently offered to sophomores (Fall, 1991).
>
> As I walk into 507, Sara, an English teacher, is looking over her notes. Soon after my arrival, she begins arranging two rows of desks into a semi-circle. Kids arrive. Many smile at me. Others ask, "Who's that?" One young man walks over to shake my hand. "Strong," he notes (Fall, 1993).

My perceptions became increasingly nuanced. For the first year, the school seemed chaotic. I tutored English 3 days a week in a small room off the cafeteria, in an area on the fifth floor which remained locked during lunch. Lunch occurred in three shifts, so I was locked in the cafeteria for 1 hour and 35 minutes, 3 days a week—an elevator ran to the fifth floor, but all stairways were blocked. Daily, teachers and students pounded on the doors to enter, and guards grew tired of unbolting the chains that fastened the doors. Once the pounding went on for what seemed like a long stretch of time. After waiting, a teacher entered reminding all who gathered around the cafeteria doors of a fire that had killed scores of people in a New York City dance club because exits had been blocked. "This," she said, "is a Happy Lands waiting to happen."

My second year at UHS (1992–1993) was easier. I saw roughly 10 students a day, a small caseload given that a counselor typically sees up to 150 teens a week and a teacher teaches 200 students a day. I spent hours discussing a single student's college essay, hours listening to a young woman's poetry. Michelle, a 15-year-old, took 45 minutes to tell me she was pregnant. She kept repeating: "I have something to say, but I know you'll be vexed with me. I know it." I asked, "What is it, Michelle?" "But you'll be vexed." After she told me about the baby, we took another hour to review a Medicaid application. I never rushed her. I did not have to; I had time.

Along with basic literacy skills, I began teaching poetry. I knew names and faces. Girls talked to me. They read their poems, their personal narratives, their essays. Kerryann, a freshman from Jamaica, showed me a marble notebook full of stories her grandfather told her. "He would hear them at the market," she said, "and then tell them over dinner."

> Candy lady, candy man.
> business bad now a days
> Lady with the pretty dress
> buy candy or go on your ways
> Nice little man, come here
> If you not buy, why you stop for?
> You move yourself
> Ya sir
> Come lady,
> Which kind you want?
> Peppermint?

It was during my second year at UHS that I worked with Hermine Meinhard through Poetry Exchange, an organization that put writers and teachers in public schools. For an hour every Wednesday, Hermine and I planned class assignments in a large classroom that had once served as an art studio. Then I watched her elicit poems from groups of teenagers in classrooms that never seemed to have enough desks. Well into middle age, Hermine looked young, almost girlish. Her girlishness suggested fragility. Her face was hidden behind horn-rimmed glasses, and when she read, her voice was barely audible. My supervisor once wondered if Hermine would gain the attention of high school teenagers—the unhidden assumption was that her size and her voice were inadequate, and that her students were too big and loud. Her raspy whisper, the effect of a viral infection, some childhood disease, has grown fainter with time. After I had been watching her teach for 2 years, she asked me if I had noticed anything different about her. I don't remember answering. "It's my voice," she said with a good deal of surprise and pleasure. "My voice is back." Months later it disappeared again, receding within her. Although she had no ability to alter volume, to soothe or cut down, this absence of a looming presence seemed to have no effect on her capacity to engage students and elicit writing. When she taught, classrooms became perfectly still, and boys once deemed remedial began to hang out in the English office.

THE POETS

I never actively, or consciously, chose the four women who became the center of this book, nor do I think of Nikki, Nessa, Jhoy, and Tanzania primarily as informants. The English assistant principal decided that two sophomore classes—an honors class and a class that drew "average" students—would make use of Hermine as a visiting poet. The average class was taught by a man who appeared a bit desperate to "get through the day." Paradoxically, Nessa was the only one of the four enrolled in this class—her poet's sensibility ignored or never perceived. Her work was often more sensuous and more powerful than that of her peers. Few others used metaphor or dialogue with greater effect. Tanzania was analytical, typical of an honors student. In the end, I talked to these women because I liked them; ethnography emerged from relationship. While revising my book, Nikki, Nessa, Jhoy, and Tanzania advised me. Tanzania read my notes and critiqued numerous versions of chapters that have since progressed to publication. Her comments changed my interpretation of ethnographic data, and they led to shifting roles: she told me to use "I" when I wrote, told me to discuss our relationship in more detail. Revision helped me cross the broad categories of age, race, and class by directing my attention to the specifics of relationship. Ultimately I came closer to young poets than I would have if I had been simply their tutor or teacher.

Nikki: "She taught me who I am"

I met Nikki the year before I started running poetry workshops. I have not seen her since 1996 but I can hear her voice when I think about her; I hear her voice before I can even see her. She has welcomed me with it, and it remained the first indication of her mood. Nikki was a happy teenager: teasing her girlfriends ("I'll miss you, heifers"), play-fighting with boys, making sure her best friend went home when her mother expected her to go home, walking along streets shuffling index cards while trying to study biology. She also seemed to fight an anger that could rise suddenly. A tutor told me, "She knocked out another girl with one punch." Sometimes the anger came from teenage anxiety: a love of home and a desire to be seen. She observed, "My father used to compare me to my friend who lived downstairs and I said, 'I can't take this. You have to stop comparing me to others.' When he does that, it feels like he wants her to be his child and not me. It's hard. My whole attitude changed. I was meaner." Sometimes it came from the need to protect herself from boys who hit her and girls who threatened her. At age 15, she defined herself through the repetitive structure of a poem.

> This is who I am
> I sit here and talk
> To myself.
> As you yell I sit and yell back not with words
> But with feelings.
>
> This is who I am
> I'm going to speak
> back and this is what
> I'm going to say: I
> can't take it anymore
> all you do is scream
> I'm not a kid anymore.
> I'm growing up. I
> want to be treated that way.
> All you make me do is go
> to school, clean, eat and sleep.

I get tired of cleaning all of the time.
You don't want to listen to me.

This is who I am
I want to be heard
I want to speak out
I need and want somebody to care for me
I want to be treated the right way.
I'm hurting inside and you don't know it.
This is who I am.

Nikki's mother, the implicit audience for "This Is Who I Am," hung the poem on the family's refrigerator door. Nikki seemed to draw strength from her, and smiled when she said: "She taught me who I am and where I'm going. My mother named me after Nikki Giavonni . . . she gave me a poet's name." And she'd grow impassioned when I interviewed her: "A lot of teachers just sit and read a book. Let us examine things—don't have us reading a book and answering questions. I want to see, feel, taste; I can't sit and do nothing." Like her poet's name, Nikki's desire to live through her senses was a gift from her mother, a woman who pushed her to leave the neighborhood and the men who hit her. After Nikki graduated from high school, her mother was still pushing. "Talk to her," she told me, "she needs a plan."

Tanzania: "I'm all lines"

People stopped Tanzania on the streets of Manhattan and told her she should become a model. That's the kind of body she had: tall, angular, with bony hands and long fingers. She never straightened her hair; she put it in braids or unraveled it—left it untouched. Years after she took her first creative writing class, Tanzie wrote "I'm All Lines." It is the best physical and psychological description of her that I can imagine.

i'm all lines and angles
no serenity here
loud throaty laughter
nothing lilting in my ways
not fine,
i'm coarse
no smooth texture
to my words

ankles and wrists
knees and elbows
knuckles
these knees won't buckle
no smooth texture
to my words

Her language served her well; like jagged teeth and the course angles of elbows, it became a shield. She once told me, "I'm afraid for those quiet girls. Don't you see that. I'm afraid for them. I can't stand to think of someone taking advantage of them. A lot of people think I'm quiet. It is true that I am quiet in school, but when I have to speak, I will. When they have to, they won't."

When the federal building in Oklahoma was bombed, I wanted to call her and listen to her reaction. I have peopled my world with folks who render an analysis quickly. She was one of them. I talked to her about events that had nothing to do with Urban High School, poetry, or Crown Heights. I wanted to listen to her. I liked the ease that settled between us. She was a friend.

Nessa: "What's wrong with being Haitian!"

I first saw Nessa in a poetry workshop. She spent the first part of the class defending herself from boys who mocked her. "Is that chain real?" one of them asked. "Yes, it is," she said. "It looks fake," another said. "No, no, it's real. It is." Her voice sounded sincere and a little sad. Hermine had asked her to incorporate dialogue into a poem. Now she sat, wrapped in a large coat, pen in front of her, not moving. I walked toward her, knowing I had the luxury of working with one kid, and talked to her about her laugh. As we talked, I took notes: jotted down what each of us said. She copied my notes, and occasionally changed a line.

Nessa, who gave you that laugh?
It's not your mother's laugh or your grandmother's
laugh.
No! It's mine.
How come you always use it?
Because it makes everybody laugh
and it makes me feel good too.
When do you laugh the most?

When somebody does something
that's not funny
I get up and laugh.
It makes everybody laugh.
Why is your laugh contagious?
Like when I was on the train with my aunt,
this man was getting up and the train was still moving,
and he fell on a whole bunch of people. I tried not to laugh
and then a few seconds later I started screaming and laughing
and yelling at the same time, I was crying because I was laugh-
ing so hard.
And then my aunt started crying of laughter
and then the whole train started laughing.
So your laughter made everyone laugh and not
the man falling?
How long did the laughter go on?
All the way home.

In 1997, the year Nessa graduated, she worked as a health care attendant, then came home and cared for her nieces. Her poetry hung on the wall of her family's living room. More than any of the other girls, Nessa's life reflects the economic and political isolation of inner cities: She has suffered the death of her mother and her grandfather; she has never seen her father. She has contributed to her family's income from the age of 15, handing over her SSI (Supplemental Security Insurance) check and then working in the service industry for less than minimum wage.

Her moods often vacillated: She would ask me, at one moment, if she could take refuge in our tutoring room and then, soon after, would scream in a school corridor or on the street. I've seen her defend Haitian students from classmates who dismissed them for being poor and dressing like "you come from a village." She'd stand up in class and scream, "What's wrong with being Haitian!" She could project her voice down a subway tunnel, but more often than not, she seemed vulnerable. "Can I stay here [the classroom where I taught poetry] today? I just don't feel like going out there." She pointed toward a crowded corridor. "I'll face it tomorrow." In a melancholy voice, she once told me she had been robbed in a local grocery store. She had gone down to the corner for a pound of bologna, when "some guy put a knife to my throat."

When I spoke of the violence in city neighborhoods, Tanzania automatically thought of Nessa. "People close to her deal drugs. . . . If we lose her completely, something good will have gone out of the world." I thought about what Tanzie said for months. I thought about losing Nessa—her laughter, her goodness. And the next time Tanzania told me she had spoken with her, I expected to hear my own fear:

> JENNIFER: What is she doing?
> TANZANIA: She's taking care of her family, I guess. But the best thing she told me is that she's still writing.
> JENNIFER: Did she bring it up or did you?
> TANZANIA: She brought it up.

Writing never erased death, drug dealing, or isolation; it never overshadowed the hours Nessa spent as a laundry attendant. But Tanzania's reference to it as "the best thing she told me" is testament to its importance, its hold over Nessa's and Tanzania's consciousness.

Jhoy: "That's how it was back home"

Jhoy clung to routines and right answers. Boys teased her, and she tried to please them. Girls dismissed her. She would never smoke a cigarette or cut a class. She was obsessed with rules. When she told Nessa and me that a guard went through her school bag and took the scissors she had used for an art project, Nessa laughed that infectious laugh. "Must have been a slow day in the hallway, if they were looking at you." In 2003, 11 years later, Nessa talked about her with empathy: "She never seemed happy with herself. She never had much confidence. I wish she had been happier. There is nothing wrong with her."

She had worn a school uniform before emigrating from St. Kitts; the regularity was comforting.

> That's how it was back home. We had a dark brown, pleated skirt, brown shirt, black shoes, white socks. That's what I wore to school everyday. I would wash them, hang them up and in the morning wear them to school.

In the United States, Jhoy skipped her graduation: "Nikki asked me why I wasn't there and I told her that I didn't pay for anything. I sat in the balcony and watched the ceremony. I didn't pay anything because it was too much money to pay." I ignored her point, her emphasis on being broke, and asked her what she remembered. She returned to the everyday hardships that I did not see and consequently dismissed, a bit too quickly.

> Well it's not actually the graduation part, but it has to do with graduating. A guy told me if I went down to Mrs. Brown or one of the people who was a head, doing the graduation, I'd be able to get a yearbook because I really wanted a yearbook if nothing else. He said there might be leftover yearbooks. I asked her if I could get a yearbook because I'm a senior. She asked me if I had paid and I said no. So she said sorry. If you paid dues, you got a yearbook [sighs].

She yearned for small things and larger ones: subway fare, college tuition, social acceptance, another body, another country. And she wrote time and again, with imagery that continually startled me. Her work was often unusual and, just as often, it was praised. "Miss Meinhard came into our English class one day and told us to write something. I wrote a poem, trying to make it good, and was very happy when I was told it was good. I was asked to keep writing, so I did." She wrote on her own after school. Her associations cut into my perceptions of conformity. I read dozens of her poems, and not one alluded to a brown skirt.

"Red Rain" exemplifies her willingness to make strange and beautiful associations; the last scenes, the lover's quarrel, brings us back to a teenage girl's desire.

RED RAIN

The red rain washed
the black birds to white doves

Look into your heart and you will see
that you are strong.
Love is said to be a sweet,
and an old fashioned notion.
Yet it scares you like a battle field.
The graceful swan isn't so graceful.
The rocky mountains aren't so rocky.
Words with a sliver streak of passion
fall from your lips onto those of your lover.

Blue lightning splits the sky.
Cold stars fall from the hearts of clouds.
You swore that you would never cry again.

Crickets cease their old love song,
as the sun writes its signature of light
across the sleeping land,
and awaken its creatures to a new day.

Inside the air has been breathed too many times.
She is asleep and in the folds
of a dying fever that makes her abdomen
feel like a quick sliver.
He is naked yet he feels covered.
As the light shines off her sunflower hair
and unto his lean tanned body.
"I'm sorry my love," he whispers into the lighting room.
He dons his clothes with painful slowness.
Wishing that the task would never end.
He turns and walks out into the smiling face of the sun.
"Don't' go."
From behind him came a muffled plea.
He keeps his back to the door and continues walking.

Since 1991, Jhoy has written poetry and prose. It took years of revisiting my notes before I could see, really see, that she was a dreamer and wrote to refashion experience. In writing this book, I crossed social and psychological boundaries and saw the particulars of her creativity. Writing brought me closer to her and the other women whose work centers this text.

RELATIONSHIP, WRITING, AND REWRITING

This book emerged from 7 years of research. As a tutor, I visited UHS three times a week for 2 years. For additional 6 months, I observed a human development class. While tutoring and observing the class, I took observational notes, describing what I saw and heard in classrooms and corridors, in counselors' and administrative offices. During my second year at UHS, I observed a poet teach two classes, again taking notes in order to understand and convey how she taught writing. I interviewed her over a period of 7 years to further understand her teaching practices and her training as a poet. I taped and transcribed hours of conversations with students and teachers and reconstructed conversations I did not tape with the school's principal, guidance counselors, and security guards. I met four young women, all students, for an additional 5 years, interviewing them in my home, at a local library, and at school. Tanzania also read my notes and versions of this work. During that 7-year period, the barrier that separates researcher and informant broke down.

There is a tension between my desire to portray the integrity of the young women who entrusted me with their stories and my obligation to mask their identity. When I told Nikki that I would have to change her name to comply with standards set by my university's Human Subject's Committee, she repeatedly said, "I will stand by what I say. Use my real name." When I asked her to sign a consent form, she read it and responded, "This doesn't get at our relationship."

The conversations cited throughout this book begin to indicate the shifting characteristics of long-term relationships, and consequence of ethnography itself. My understanding and subsequent use of the term "ethnography" in this context stems from anthropologist Karen Brown's definition of ethnographic research as a form of human relationship that brings intellectual labor and life into closer relation (Brown, 1991, p. 12). My friendship with Nessa, Nikki, and Jhoy has shaped this book, but my relationship with Tanzania has brought work and life into closer relation. Hours after giving birth to my son, I thought of her; she has appeared in my dreams and she has made me forget some of the monotonous details of my own life.

In retrospect, I remember her honesty. Maintaining that honesty was difficult—at least for me. When teenage anxiety, or exuberance, became exhausting, I fantasized about severing my relationship to Tanzie or Jhoy. In one of my dreams, teenagers burst into my apartment, my bedroom, laughing, spilling over each other like children. I became tired of their energy, their spontaneity, and wanted to be alone, wanted a place they could not enter. At other times, I clung to my own fear, hesitant to leave Manhattan.

> Listening to the evening news, a day before I plan to walk down
> Flatbush with Tanzie, I hear about the violence that surrounds her.
> A young man is caught in cross fire when police shoot at someone
> wielding a knife. The following day, I spoke with Tanzie three
> times. She asked me to come to a subway station near Flatbush.

After two additional calls, I told her to meet me closer to
Manhattan. "I'll arrive faster, I'll know the route." I never said that
I was afraid to come directly into her neighborhood. Never admit-
ted it. Perhaps it was a mixture of pride and a refusal to point to
the differences between us that caused me to remain silent.

Fixed class distinctions separated me from Tanzania and every other teen
who enrolled at UHS. They surfaced through material reality. While visiting
my apartment, Nessa said: "Your doors are locked, the intercom works.
Nice." On another occasion, she told me that my neighbors were hesitant to
let her into the building: "How many Black people live here?" Older Black
men and women do live in my building. Teens are a rarer sight, regarded with
suspicion. Urban High School students visited New York University, the
school I attended, while I tutored them, but few were academically prepared
to go there and even fewer were able to afford it. Yet the nature of my rela-
tionship with the four women was defined in the moment and forged in dis-
tinctly different locations. When I worked with Tanzania on her college essay,
my interaction with her was influenced by years of teaching composition and
rhetoric at a prestigious university. When she took me through her neigh-
borhood, when she ordered Haitian pastry for the two of us, when she
responded to my observational notes, power relations shifted; she suggested
and occasionally shaped the course of narration.

> TANZANIA: You're writing a book? Call Nessa. She has a lot to say.
> JENNIFER: I don't feel comfortable talking about the fact that her
>   mother died, that Subbie [an aunt] and Nessa are trying to
>   hold everything together.
> TANZANIA: Maybe she wants the recognition. She was a girl, a girl
>   [voice becomes louder] who had to be the parent. Perhaps see-
>   ing her story in print is the only way she'll be remembered.
> JENNIFER: Is she [Nessa] still in school?
> TANZIE: I didn't ask. I don't want to ask all these questions over the
>   phone. I want to sit down and look at her.

She bears witness, recognizes the value of story: "Perhaps seeing it in
print is the only way [Nessa] will be remembered." Yet she returns to rela-
tionship—reminding me that "getting the story" is secondary to her concern
for Nessa. I will ultimately get a story—pen it down. But I, too, have sat
down with Nessa and listened to her. And sitting down with her has made it
difficult to theorize poverty and loneliness. Tanzie noticed the difficulty.

From 1992 to 1999, our roles as listener and storyteller shifted. I remember sitting around my kitchen table with Tanzania, Nessa, and Jhoy, while Nessa talked about the death of an uncle.

NESSA: I try to be good to my aunt but I don't like what's happening in my house. That's why I've been running the streets.
 I can't take it no more it's just me and my aunt. My uncle died. My aunt has been with my other uncle since she was fifteen. They have five kids and me. I watched my mother die. I saw it. We all saw it.

Later in the day, Tanzania came to me and said, "It [Nessa's story] will fester inside you and you'll come to me and tell me you're sad." I carry the burden of a story until I release it by confessing why I am sad. Tanzie not only conceptualized her role as a listener, she saw behind my silence and understood that by breaking the silence, I could find redemption. Her understanding came from close observation of me, which always entailed a close reading of my writing.

Ongoing discussions about my writing caused me to reassess my perceptions of UHS, Crown Heights, and my relationship to UHS students. After reading a final revision of "Aesthetic Safety Zones," [1] a book chapter in which I describe the schooling practices at UHS, Tanzania said: "You never say that students disrupted other students. There were times when I wished security guards had entered the classroom." In response to her readings, my research has become more porous. When I feel hesitant, I return to her and grapple with my representations of her neighborhood, her school, and herself. Sometimes she'd turn the focus on me. When she first read a draft of the book chapter, she responded: "I have three questions: Why were you there? What made you decide to spend hours with us? Why were you interested? And use 'I' when you tell this story."

Over the 7 years I have known her, she has watched the eye of an observer/writer, guiding it, acknowledging its importance. "Are you going to write about that?" "What?" "Don't you see it? Look at where my foot is." By drawing my attention to the crack vials in her neighborhood, Tanzania directed my observation and created a particular kind of witness. And after years of give and take, my writing began to reflect the particulars of our relationship. She criticized an early draft of "Aesthetic Safety Zones" for not accurately reflecting the give and take of our daily interaction: "Look at all these dates. You've known me for years, but reading this I get the impression that you imposed yourself, you put yourself in my neighborhood. You didn't. When

did I get your phone number?" I do not remember giving her my number—
it was so long ago. So her interpretative comments are embedded in this text
and my perceptions are embedded in her reflections. The ensuing reciproci-
ty has leveraged my voice, enabling an ethnographic methodology girded by
revision. Once I asked her to elaborate on a comparison she had made
between scanning and a man's gaze: "Are the two similar because you do not
know how you are being looked at?" In her response, I heard the echo of my
own questions: "There is a difference. Before I saw him staring at me I felt
free. . . . With the scanning, I knew how to be. I knew not to be free.
[Seconds of silence] And now you'll ask me what I mean by free." Her reply
called up the roles we were playing at the moment; it delineated them and
perhaps inverted them. She reminded me that there are differences between
normal conversation and the probing, reflective conversation between
informant and ethnographer, between interviewer and interviewee. Tanzie
made me her subject-object by invading or predicting my words and
thoughts, yet she still answered my question.

Performing multiple roles comes after years of reading her my notes,
transcripts, and the drafts of numerous papers. She has watched my eye. She
knows my language.

> JENNIFER: Do they [the guards] stop more boys than girls?
> TANZANIA: I think it was more boys than girls. Actually there was
>   more commotion on the boys' line than the girls'. More play-
>   fulness on the boys' line. The girls just wanted to get it done.
>   Maybe the boys playing around means they're uncomfortable
>   too. We just don't say anything but the boys do. (March 1995)

Elaboration—June, 1995

> JENNIFER: What were you thinking when you said this?
> TANZANIA: Both girls and boys were uncomfortable. We were silent
>   in our own defense. That's how you would say it. [She laughs]
>   I just wanted to get upstairs. It was a mute button. Being
>   silent wouldn't prolong the invasion. I'd stare at them [the
>   guards]. I wanted to know at any point if they got any pleasure
>   out of it. That's why they would hurry to get away from my
>   stare. [Laughs] At least I would make them uncomfortable and
>   that made me feel better. Would you say that I was invading
>   them just as much as they were invading me?

"We were silent in our own defense. That's how you would say it." The sentence conveys reflexivity. It recalls: "And now you'll ask me what I mean by free." The transference of subject-object positions did of course break down when I wrote this text. As James Clifford reminds us: "While ethnographies cast as encounters between two individuals may successfully dramatize the intersubjective give-and-take and introduce a counterpoint of authorial voices, they remain representations of dialogue" (Clifford, 1988, p. 43). Representations of authority do not permanently alter ethnographic authority. Tanzania is a student, a friend, a perceptive critic. She is also the subject of this book, a book I ultimately shaped. My representations of our conversation and daily interaction did not always successfully portray their complex, evolving nature, yet writing augmented and, in some cases, caused a complex, evolving relationship.

As a writing teacher, I insisted that she not simply witness, but also document what she sees. Once she told me that some of the young men in her neighborhood spent their days standing on a street corner, and then lamented that no one has written about it.

> TANZANIA: I told Christian, my neighbor, to write about it because no one is writing about it. [She accents the final phrase, raising the pitch of her voice to enunciate "because" and "writing." She then lowers her voice and repeats] No one has written about it.
> JENNIFER: You write about it—it's your neighborhood.

Once more, our roles are inverted as different personas emerge within the relationship. I now know these personas (oral storyteller/listener, informant/observer, guiding eye/researcher) emerged through writing. As a poet, Tanzania has become an observer, a researcher of her own life world; and as a teacher, I have asked that she continue writing. By witnessing the marginalization of men who stand outside a mainstream labor force, by documenting their lives and by insisting that their lives be documented, she ensures their visibility. She and her peers honed their voices and artistic sensibilities in school: They narrated their own lives, they used language in unusual ways, and they created an order that remained with them even outside UHS. Hermine helped her students feel the genre's power, its diverse potential, by showing them how to wield language and lose themselves in it. In her workshops they, too, crossed social and psychological boundaries—her assignments set students on both a conscious and unconscious search for the most complex part of themselves.

I HAD THE KNACK FOR POETRY

I had the knack for poetry. It was in me. I just needed
someone to bring it out.
—Nessa, January 10, 1999

I heard Hermine read "Teacher," one of her poems, in 1998. Years later she said that she believed the poem articulated "what I would want for my students, to internalize a guiding voice that helps them to claim parts of themselves."

TEACHER

you, holding this thing up to me
                    fractured   the way I always was

        for a long time frightened

but I was waiting   for what would then be you
            a small awkwardly shaped mountain
            that you held up to me

        You want me to be lonely
the way the animals are   thinking in this way
            that I will come to know you

wanting the same quiet strength the mountain had
                floating like a character in a dream

        but if you find me wild like that, I will already be
            a voice in the mountain

where then will you be?
—Hermine Meinhard

To write the poem, she worked with a dream image: "A friend was holding a mountain in his hand, urging me to look at it. I felt he was urging me to look at my own value. I worked with the image in my notebook, not knowing where it would take me." Hermine taught the way she wrote the poem, moving from an image, "not knowing where it would take me." She gave her students material—objects that seemed wildly dissimilar, photographs, language—but would not direct them into a specific subject. Like the mountain image in her dream, Hermine's material worked as a starting point from which students explored initial impulses, and found their individuality. To teach this way, intuitively, she had to trust her students' sensibilities, the way she trusted her own. She had to believe they could write poetry. And they did.

Hermine perceived the process of writing as an effort to connect with original or primary material and, therefore, never rushed to revise new work. She feared that efforts to "clean up" one's writing could extinguish the spark: "You run the risk of draining the life from it." Her models were artists like Charles Olson, poets who attempt to convey the energy and chaos in the mind. Olson privileged the shape of perception, rather than the external ideas of form. "Keep moving," he advised, "keep in, speed, the nerves, their speed, the perceptions, theirs, the acts, the split second acts, the whole business, keep it moving as fast as you can, citizen" (1966, p. 17). Hermine took his advice. Consequently it appeared as if she called forth images that were always there. She stated: "My emphasis was not on form. I wanted students to create from their own experience, and leading with form might have impeded their ability to connect to personal language and experiences." She never scanned student poetry; she never imposed order on language. Instead, she worked improvisationally, eliciting a kind of creative disorder. She credited her own teacher, Ruth Danon, for shaping the way she taught: "My teacher taught by having us write in class. She gave us material that acted as stimuli, and provided a container within which there was great freedom. Her constraints were never subject based but allowed writers to discover their own subjects; they enabled us to go beyond restrictions, usual ways of thinking." Outside her workshops, guards walked the corridors with walkie-talkies. Occasionally they entered classrooms to remove students—interrupting a space that still held the promise of sanctuary.

I once heard her talk about "the place where I learned to follow whatever images were inside me." Jhoy and I had attended a reading in the basement of a café, and she introduced herself, her writer's self, through a New York City neighborhood: "I live in a very humble apartment in a part of the city that was once known as the Hungarian section. It is a very small apartment overlooking a church parking lot—where there is a particular tree. Sometimes that tree allows me to fool myself into believing I live over a courtyard. This is the place where I became a writer." She reads a poem about entering the tree's shadow, moving in and out of darkness. I left the reading thinking about transcendence: the poet who looks at a tree and sees a space that is more beautiful than it is.

At UHS, Hermine evoked the fragments of memory and urged students to weave an aesthetic whole from the various pieces of their own experience. She brought in the work of poets who valued memory and kept a map of the African diaspora in their heads. Students read "Holding":

> She braids them again, obeying
> a tradition in Ghana, in Guinea
> in a D.C. home business so skilled in
> managing three worlds of hair, blending
> them into one unit of braid without
> juggling or favoring
> —Thylias Moss, from *Callaloo*, Winter 1993

And after they read, Hermine's voice rasped: "How do identities affect storytelling? Are stories from home told or are they left behind? Who keeps the old stories alive? Are identities at war with each other? Do you feel like you have to throw everything away? Your language? Your stories? Tell the stories your grandmother told you."

Kerryann did not need to be told to write in Creole. She had written her grandfather's stories in a marble notebook before she ever met Hermine. And Gerald, a second-generation immigrant from Haiti, imagined characters who dreamt of Haitian goddesses in a story entitled "Kachimbo" (or "pipe"):

> When I was a child I dreamt of spitting on Erzulie Freda
> When I was a child I dreamt of marrying Erzulie Danto
> As I grew of age I wanted to marry the sea,
> Yemanya, ayiboo Erzulie, Ayibobo Danto.
> When I became a man, I grew into the day and remembered
> my promise.
> I spit at the dark, I spit at the light for it was fortune that
> decreed that we could not return to Dahomey, for it was for-
> tune that made me spit each night, each night I spit at the pic-
> ture of Danto watching my back jolt sideways to silence the
> rhythm of memories—Oh Gede, Oh Ibo, Oh Ago!!!
> Oh Ibo the misery of spitting makes me want to flee

Rituals of return and the desire to flee help define the main character.

> GERALD: Dahomey is the ancestral home of Voudou spirits in Haitian folklore; slaves of Hispanola would sing to and return to Dahomey; it was a place where they were free of all problems and progress. In [the first poem] of [Kachimbo] spitting is a metaphor which conveys a longing to depart from life's pain and return to Dahomey.

"Kachimbo" was replete with images of Haitian land and Haitian people: "There were people who came from Font Rouge and their feet were always red because the earth itself was red; no matter how much they washed, they were still red." Gerald anchored the story's imagery and its metaphors "in the idea of universal suffrage and the foundation of a home." Like Kerryann, he threw nothing away.

Students wrote consistently in Hermine's class, and they wrote well. By creating experiences that allowed students to go beyond constraints and by making a "safe container," she became a catalyst for good writing. "Take us back to the place you remember. Close your eyes. Does it take you back? What do you see, taste, feel?" Some, like Kenneth, crossed an ocean and went "home."

HOME

The green trees, the small stream, wanting
to get out from bed, to feel the sun on my face and walk on
the wet grass, to eat a mango
still wet and cold from morning.
Looking forward to the new day ahead, to finishing my chores
before my breakfast was ready.
In the kitchen the smell of hot homemade bread and fish cakes
made me work faster. Then my friends will pass, calling. Calling
me at the top of their voices.
It was time to leave the house, putting my unfinished breakfast
into my pocket and my shoes in my hands. I will escape
through the back window, running as fast as I can, ignoring
my mother's call.

Like all writers, like all human beings, Kenneth construes his experience in the past as another part of the self—a self viewed through time, or what Salman Rushdie (1991) refers to as the "shards of memory." These shards "acquire greater status, greater resonance because they are remains" that give meaning to the present (p. 12).

We all look back through the broken remnants of time, we all emigrate from the past (Rushdie, 1991) and in the process we lose pieces of ourselves. Immigrants, however, experience an actual physical loss and thus seem to savor the remains of memory far more intensely than those of us who never move from the place where we were born. The sensuality of Kenneth's language—"a mango still wet and cold from morning"—conveys the absolute joy of going home.

Students also wrote within the constraints of time and place, responding to the immediacy of the present. Hermine asked them to draw a picture of a place that was important, list all the objects in that place and then write about it, opening with "When I got there, everything had changed . . . " Nadia wrote about a shooting incident in her neighborhood.

> When I got there everything had changed
> The school bus was parked over the
> garden, with kids running through the flowers.
> There were cars driving fast as lightening,
> VOOM, VOOM
> They were all making frightening noises
> The store was bigger than it was
> With colors and streaks and Graffiti
> There were gang fights all through
> The neighborhood with knives and guns
> They took. Slash. They waved their knives
> Bang. They shot their guns. The sounds became
> dangerous   everyone was quiet.

Teens captured their vision of the events they witnessed in school, at home, and on the street in spiral notebooks. Tanzania's notebook was "big, messy. I never associated it with school." These books, decorated with thick markers, became *the place* to record and reflect on lived experience. Teens kept them close to their bodies, assertively writing their names on the covers.

As almost sacred objects, notebooks became a place for honesty, or what Tanzie called "truth."

> I remember walking around with a notebook, ready to write down what I had seen. I remember being with my father, after church. He was bringing me home in a taxi. We stopped in front of a club, and waited for the light to turn green. I saw a huge group of people outside that club and I thought they were waiting to get in, until I heard the sound of the gunfire. The shots didn't sound real to me; I have defined TV as reality and TV sounds different than gunfire in my face. I wanted to get home and write about how black men are killing each other; I wanted to tell on them. I wanted to tell God. (Tanzania, December 1997)

By shaping memory and recording events in her notebook, Tanzania learned habits of observation and narration that allowed her to exercise a kind of control over her world: "Writing gave me freedom" (June 1998). It also provided her with another reason to notice and remember what she had seen. She subsequently developed an eye for detail and narrative shapes, and through these details and the line of a story, she chose when to remain silent and when to speak.

> I had been angry for so long about black on black violence, but on that night when I sat next to my father violence wasn't distant anymore. My father was there. My father could have been hurt and that alone makes me angry. If ever my family is threatened in anyway, there is nothing I can do but be furious, but tell, but scream.

Tanzania watched events around her, told God, and temporarily imposed order on the outside world with a desire "to get home and write." Her willingness to both "tell God" and "write down" reveals the intimate nature of poetry and the need to grapple with physical uncertainty. Dredging words from silence before God becomes a prayer that enters the public realm. Like prayer, poetry has the effect of holding the world together, of connecting internal and external life, of articulating and making stable what is not (Norris, 1998, p. 58). Through an appropriation of imagery, Tanzania vacillates between social madness and internal rage.

Ultimately, Hermine's suggestion that students record what they see prompted Tanzania to write about the horror of violent death. By placing a private self within a social landscape, by allowing the reader to look at that sphere of her life, to judge it, to assess it, she offers herself up as an object of reflection, but she also narrates her own anger, and asks that we listen. Bearing witness to atrocities and then railing against them through poetry became a means of defining and redefining experience. Moreover, writing forged and reinforced Tanzie's belief that her perceptions were worth telling, and thus lead to a kind of psychic resilience.

By privileging both literal and metaphorical references, the real, the remembered, and the imagined, Hermine helped students hold onto the images of childhood, moments of rueful laughter and painful reverie. These moments rarely came together as a seamless narrative. They were disjunctive, shifting so suddenly that the reader perceived the rendered experience from different, even contradictory angles. Hermine's own strategy, as both teacher and writer, was to bring up the unconscious. She pushed herself and her students to make nonrational and nonassociational leaps, allowing the unconscious to come into the work.

As a writer I have conflicting impulses: to tell a story and to put down words in an idiosyncratic or associational way. I will begin with a table. Now you might expect family to gather around that table as food appears and the table is set. But I will place the table in a desert and work with that. (Hermine Meinhard, "To Know by Heart," presented at The Kitchen, February 10–11, 1999)

She introduced her students to the poetry of surrealists and discussed the logic of dreams, believing that the surreal world is connected to the deeper workings of consciousness, and that this connection provides access to another part of the self (H. Meinhard, personal communication, July 8, 1999). In one class she told her students to imagine a physical metamorphosis, to pretend, to close their eyes to "see beings become plants, animals." Terms like "metamorphosis" and "transformation" were reinforced through group writing. Students were invited to transform themselves and others. They volunteered ideas that were written on the board.

They fight with automatic weapons,
a razor, a machete. They drink malt liquor.
Smoking reefers. Lots of graffiti on the wall.
They change into fawns.

The collective effort drew on a perception of the "real" and the imagined. This exercise created an experience to which all responded. By asking her students to transcend sensation, Hermine enabled them to perceive what is possible. She consequently taught them the power of creativity and allowed them to write and speak beyond the limits of physical space and daily routine. Through surrealist fantasy, writers made alternative truths. They moved from the external constraints of their lives: the locked doors, the barbed-wire fences, the pull of social conventions, the demands of relationship. Attention to nonrational experiences enabled them to bring a range of psychological states into their work: mourning, violent impulses, total alienation, and a desire for care. These states led to writing that often altered the way they were represented in school corridors and on neighborhood streets.

Once she asked sophomores to read "Tonton Makout," a poem that is embedded in a specific place and time—they saw Haiti during François Duvalier's authoritarian rule (1957–1971)—and then she gave them "Abandoned Church," a poem that pushes us beyond what is rational and already known.

TONTON MAKOUT

A boy was going to play
He climbed out on a tree branch
His mama told him to come down
A passing tonton makout asked her
"Do you want me to bring him down for you"
He drew his pistol and killed the boy
—Felix Momsseau-Leroy

ABANDONED CHURCH
(BALLAD OF THE GREAT WAR)

Once I had a son named John.
Once I had a son.
He was lost in the arches, one Friday, Day of the Dead.
I saw him playing on the last raised steps of the Mass
And he lowered a tin bucket into the priest's deep heart
I pounded on coffins. My son! My son! My son!
—Federico García Lorca

After reading, she took her students through a series of visceral exercises: imagine yourself becoming extremely small and extremely large. Finally, she asked them to close their eyes and leap to an imagined place or a place they know—Jhoy wrote "I Believe."

In the poem, place becomes surreal, suggesting a flight into fantasy. The work's mixture of real and imagined scenes enables the writer to create a place and a self that are separate from reductive routines. Jhoy is so often confined to household drudgery, caretaking responsibilities, minimum-wage jobs—the day-to-day hand-to-mouth living that saps creative energy. She has, momentarily, transcended her own life.

I BELIEVE

1.
I believe in New York Nights.
I have never slept in Manhattan.
I went to a show,
And saw two men on stage,

They danced and spun in the air.
They were naked.
They were painted blue.

2.
Cold raindrops fall onto the streets of Paris.
I stop walking and look down the street.
I see a pink mist floating towards me,
Through the gray haze of the rain.
It stops two feet away from me.
Red lips peak out from under a large pink hat.
They asked me a question.
I said yes.
"You lie," they said.
They were supported by a pink dress,
And pink pumps.
I never lie.

3.
I am walking home along the street Broadway.
I'm walking home from a movie,
An old black and white one.
I always go to the movies alone.
A brown mouse of a man passes me by.
He possesses the scent of coconut oil.
It waffles off him and onto me.
Now the smell lingers on my body.

4.
"You have a world of happiness,
My world is one of existence."
I told him to touch me.
Am I not in his world?
"Are you not the half of the flesh and blood that make me
     whole?
How can you say that my world is one of happiness,
When you are no part of it?"
He gathers me up into his arms,
And buries his head into my blue sweater,
And starts to cry.

I wrap my arms around his head,
And whisper things to assure him that the world isn't so bad.
I look out the window and watch the rain fall.

Jhoy distinguishes two cities through an exterior/interior divide. New York is a place where men dance naked on stage. In Paris, love and the strange are inside the city's people. On its streets, someone, perhaps a couple, sees inside the writer—inside her poetic fantasy lie. New York City veers away from the stage in stanza four, when Jhoy speaks to and embraces a man, but within this solitary place there are still two worlds—one of happiness, the other of existence.

Despite her admission "My world is one of existence," Jhoy rarely wrote about a concrete reality. Instead, she wrote about the bodies of her imaginary lovers. She found images in newspaper clippings and refashioned herself:

Before my eyes I watch countries
Become battlegrounds.
My eyes are lovely meadows turned into a place where
The dead live.
Glistening marble tombstones stand in the place of daisies.

Jhoy's writing often emerged from the interplay between her own internal reality and her control of actual objects. Hermine encouraged this kind of play, relying on props to stimulate the imagination. She once told me that masks tend to bring up images buried under the layers of a life: "They have a strong connection to the unconscious."

Through an exercise that literally required students to put on a mask, Tanzie considered the flexibility of individual identity; she sloughed off perceptions of how she was perceived and became free to discover multiple ways of being.

I always thought about how many masks I present to the world. When Miss Meinhard asked us to write through a mask, I was able to write through many masks. I remember asking who [what part of myself] do I want to show. I remember drawing a happy and a sad face alongside my poem. Here were the doors I'd been dying for. By presenting the mask, Miss Meinhard allowed me to recognize that I have a mask, that everyone has masks. She was the only one who asked me to do what I wanted. Finally, some adult gave me what I wanted.

Doors that lead to the donning of multiple personas free the writer of social and psychological restrictions, allowing her to discover some other part of herself.

Despite awareness—the realization that one wears many masks—Tanzie, Jhoy, Nessa, and Nikki wrote themselves into a kind of individualized permanence. By isolating introspection or social awareness on a page, poetry constructs identities (selves, personas) which are then recognized by others. Writing encourages a sense of closure, "a sense that what is found in a text has been finalized, has reached a state of completion" (Ong, 1982, p. 132). Each young woman collected her own verse over an extended period of time—preserving it in homemade books and files. The poems became objects that remained after fleeting perceptions, and the act of writing over time created a sense of constancy. Five years after I first met Nessa, I asked her if I could see some new work. Minutes after we met on a corner in Manhattan, she showed me two poems, carefully wrapped in a plastic file. After reading one, I asked her why she continued to write. "I just like it," she said.

She passed her poem to me and then to Tanzania, allowing us to move closer to her. Her words are intimate:

To feel your fingertips up and down my back
To feel your hands run through my hair with a slight pull

Yet Nessa writes to move into a social world. When we asked her why she wrote the poem, she told us:

I was just sitting there and thinking about my relationship and life;
and I thought others would view their own relationships like I
view mine.

She writes to forge connections. Her permanence is embedded in the creation of an object, wrapped, saved, and repeatedly touched, and it is embedded in the relationships that her writing evokes.

NOTE

1. "Aesthetic Safety Zones" appears in *Construction Sites*, a compilation of essays edited by Lois Weis and Michelle Fine (2000).

CHAPTER 2

Discard and Permanence in Postindustrial New York

Stay in high school.
Go to college, unlike I did.
Get a good job
So you won't sometimes have
To depend on others.
—"Housekeeper," Nessa, 1992

Stretches of Flatbush Avenue look like a Caribbean oasis. Stores sell dishes that I have never heard of, some that I have seen, but never eaten: cow foot, roti, meat wrapped in dough, tripe and beans, curry goat. As I sit in one restaurant eating Jamaican patties, I am surrounded by entertainment flyers specific to a West Indian audience. *Scandal, Lies and a Visa: A Caribbean Comedy* is scheduled for a local theater. Outside, religious men hawk Bibles and salvation near vendors who sell nuts wrapped in cellophane. Sermons in Haitian Creole seep through storefront churches, and women market African jewelry in front of Brooklyn's oldest church. From my position across the broad street, they appear to work directly underneath a white steeple. The color and human activity of the market overwhelm the older church, reducing it to a backdrop. In retrospect, I see that the women who market in this space have become the bearers of economic viability; they live off their own vibrancy—talking, enticing people to pause near the street. At the very least, they are symbols of possibility. Further down the block, on the side of a Caldor, someone has written "slice cops." As we turn the corner, I ask Tanzie to describe the neighborhood we are entering. She replies, "One of those industrial neighborhoods, abandoned cars, stripped of their parts." The area seems less alive. No vendors.

FURTHER DOWN THE BLOCK

Next to the laughter and the markets of Crown Heights lie broken cars: images that convey the social and economic marginalization of the city's working class and of its poor. Within blocks of a vibrant market stands a row of boarded-up brick buildings; one of them has been vacant for as long as anyone can remember. "My grandmother can't remember when it wasn't abandoned," said one teen. Neighborhoods "stripped of their parts" have become the inevitable conclusion of social neglect, and a reflection of disposability. Kashan, A UHS sophomore, writes movingly about the ravages of capital flight and the crack epidemic, which swept through New York in the 1980s. Public and private disinvestment began to sap her childhood neighborhood of its vitality in the mid-1970s, and when crack became New York's drug of choice, her working-class neighbors did not have sufficient resources to protect the addict or her children. The ensuing social effects were still visible when Kashan entered high school in 1991.

> I landed on top of a roof. I can't place where but it looks familiar. The buildings are old & worn out. They look black from fires. The stores have no lights, the windows are broken & the posters are torn. I go to the next building, I see smoke coming out of a window. At first I thought it was a fire but I noticed a man with a pipe in his hand. Then I heard children crying, these people were smoking crack. Now I see why the neighborhood is ruined. It is like this because of the drug dealers & drug users. Now I know where I am: "This is my old neighborhood."

The passage itself, specifically the line "Then I heard children crying," reminds us of the single most devastating effect on corporate avarice, public disinvestment, and the addict's insatiable need for the drug: the physical and emotional abandonment of children.

For a number of people in Crown Heights, marginalization has replaced labor exploitation as a dominant form of oppression. As marginals, the friends, neighbors, and family members of UHS students have become "people the system of labor cannot or will not use" (Young, 1990, p. 53). In 1990, the year before I started tutoring at Urban High School, unemployment in the surrounding area was 13%. An additional 29% of the population was not in the labor force. This figure reflects men and women who did not or could not work: the elderly, children, the disabled, prisoners, and discouraged workers, those who had stopped looking for work. People in the last group

may have been out of a job for years, but because they were no longer regis-
tered with an unemployment office, their number is hard to discern.
Tanzania describes the effect of unemployment on the young men in her
neighborhood:

> There are these guys on the corner of my block. They stand there
> all day. That's all they do. They stand on the corner and they
> smoke reefer. And I know they want to move but they can't.
> (Fieldnotes, February 1995)

Without work, it becomes difficult, if not impossible, to move from one
structured routine to another. Life's rhythm, as it has been defined by indus-
trial society, breaks down (Wilson, 1996, p. 73). Entry into the city's bureau-
cracies—its welfare, social security, and unemployment offices, or, as my
example below illustrates, its court system—further undermines the pre-
dictability of the ticking of the clock. Dependence on the state for support
or services leaves one open to the whims of a bureaucrat.

Nessa spent hours in one social welfare office or another, waiting to fill
out forms. Orphaned as a child, she was entitled to state money, and pursued
that money to support her family. As Tanzania once insisted, she shouldered
adult responsibilities: "You know how she received money from the govern-
ment? So many times that money kept the family from being evicted"
(Fieldnotes, December 1997). Dependency led to oppression.

> NESSA: I have to go to the SSI office Friday.
> JENNIFER: For a job? [I had agreed to meet her at the Door, a
>   youth agency, on Friday. She told me that she was looking for
>   work and the agency had a job opportunity program.]
> NESSA: No. Remember I told you I get a check every month. I was
>   told that the checks will be cut off on my eighteenth birthday
>   because I'd be out of school. I have to go to show that I'll be
>   in school.
> JENNIFER: Well, call me if you want to go to the Door Friday.
>   Sometimes going to the SSI office takes all day.
> NESSA: I know, right. I'll call you. [Nessa won't call. She will go to
>   the SSI office. Wait on line. Interact with case workers. Fill out
>   forms. It will take an entire day.] (Fieldnotes, June 1995)

Nessa relies on a welfare agency to support her family, so she waits to
show a case worker she's in school. While waiting, she is not in school and

she is not looking for work. And while waiting, she internalizes the notion that her time has no value. By age 16, Nessa had become a patient woman. Unlike Tanzania, she never complained when she waited to enter UHS. Waiting stemmed from and reinforced her marginality. While in high school, it was all too often her norm.

I stepped into a world where time was not predictable in criminal court, when I bailed a friend out of prison. In this place, where life is wasted, I felt dehumanized and began to see how easily we internalize routine contempt:

> Jimmy was arrested for assault and on Wednesday, August eighth, Karen and I went to his arraignment. We were one of the few Whites in court. Most of the people waiting for friends or family were Black; some were Latina. One woman cried. Earlier in the day I repeatedly called Central Booking. No one could tell me when Jim would be arraigned. They told me it would likely be that night. When I arrived at nine, the judge was on break. I was told she'd return at eleven, so I walked to a diner and waited. She did return at eleven and set bail. I took money from my bank account and went to the courthouse, thinking I could pay a clerk and go home. We are sent to another building, the tombs, a temporary prison for men and women on their way to Rikers.
>
> Roughly ten people are in a small room; others wait outside. One man had been waiting for his son since three in the afternoon. At one in the morning on the following day, he was still waiting. Many of the people waiting with us—people I'd talk to over the next 6 hours—had been in the system before: they knew how to post bail, they knew how long guards would keep defendants before shipping them off to Rikers, they knew how paperwork slowed after bail officers changed shifts. "Waiting to post bail," said one, "is like waiting to see a judge; it's like doing time all over again."

After waiting from 12:00 a.m. to 6:00 a.m. to complete paperwork, I was exhausted, but went home to take care of my 12-month-old son. I also scrubbed my bathroom floor and took two showers, trying to distance myself from contempt and an absolute dismissal of my time, as much as from the flies that circled a bail room. Wait for 6 hours to fill out three forms, and you begin to feel that your time is not important. Wait repeatedly and, on some level, you must come to believe that you are expendable. Waiting not only assumes marginality, it begins to define a world in which human beings are "expelled from useful participation in social life and thus potentially subjected to severe material neglect" (Young, 1990, p. 53).

Disposability characterizes marginalization, which, according to Iris Marion Young, is "perhaps the most dangerous form of oppression" (1990, p. 53). For other theorists, human wastage is the face of a distinctly American capitalism, visible "in a country where to waste is the common criminal slang for 'to kill'" (Hobsbawm, 2003). David Harvey argues that consumerism underscores the dynamics of a throw-away society, which "meant more than throwing away produced goods, but also being able to throw away values, lifestyles, stable relationships, and attachments to things, buildings, places, people, and received ways of doing and being" (Harvey, 1989, p. 286). On city streets, Harvey's "throw-away" metaphor echoes American slang; it refers directly to human life, human wastage. After displaying scores of photographs depicting the scarred bodies of gang members to a university audience, one of Manhattan's assistant district attorneys smiled and said, "Do you know what drug carriers are called—Dixie cups. They're the industry's throw-away people" (Arsenault, 1997). The personal consequences of this kind of oppression, of complete disregard for human life and dignity, are devastating, and all too evident in Nessa's life and in the lives of the other poets.

> NESSA: I need a job. I have done badly in my classes. I haven't shown up. I got a Z in one class.
> JENNIFER: What does that mean?
> NESSA: Never showed up. He doesn't make much money and he's got five kids and me. [Her voice becomes louder with the last two words.] The rent's backing up. They're going to turn off our phone. I have to pay for some of these bills. I have done that before. I have paid for the lights. But I can't just pay for house bills. I need boots. I need to pay for my own things. [She seems tired. Weighted. Her eyelids droop.]
> JENNIFER: [I have no idea how to respond.] Will you talk to someone else about this?
> NESSA: I've told Sharon. I haven't told Nikki. Just don't feel like it, you know.
> JENNIFER: Have you told your aunt what you have told me?
> NESSA: Yeah.
> JENNIFER: What does she do?
> NESSA: She cries. (Fieldnotes, October 1994)

We see in the above exchange Nessa's financial burden, born of material deprivation, but more overwhelmingly, we sense a horrible loneliness. Nessa told me this story 10 minutes after I sat down with her in a crowded tutoring room. I had not seen her in 6 months. Looking back, there seems to be so few places where she could have gone for support. I have come to believe that loneliness, more than any other state, aptly characterizes marginalization's effect on children. Within this context, poetry became an expression of one's social circumstances and a means to write against the concept of a throw-away society. By writing against discard, Nessa celebrated her connection to the one person who has never left her, her aunt Subbie. Thus, by writing, she asserted her own humanity and her connection to another human being as well as reclaimed her dignity.

Thirteen percent of the residents who lived in Crown Heights were unemployed in 1990. Countless others were overworked. Economic uncertainty seemed to underscore the sense that you could rely on no one. According to Nessa's aunt Subbie, economic dependence was a trap. Following is the poem "Housekeeper" in its entirety.

HOUSEKEEPER

Wash the dishes
Do your homework
Wash the clothes
Cook dinner
Make up your bed
Please watch the kids.
Take them to the park to ride their bikes.
Don't let anybody pressure you to have sex.
Don't stay out too late.
Don't talk about people.
I am saying all of this
So you will know what to
do when you grow up and have kids.
Stay in high school.
Go to college, unlike I did.
Get a good job
So you won't sometimes have
To depend on others.
—Nessa, 1992

Nessa stayed in high school, but did not go to college as Subbie advised. In 1999, she worked as a laundry attendant and as a clerk in a 99-cent store. Sometimes she worked 7 days a week, yet she struggled to pay for housing, electricity, and health care. She was not alone. In 1997, 74% of all students attending UHS were eligible for free lunch. By the year 2000, that number had risen to 78% (The 1999–2000 Annual School Report Card, issued by the New York City Board of Education Division of Assessment and Accountability). The financial strain on UHS families, on an underemployed service sector, is evident in "Housekeeper," a poem with the same title as Nessa's, but written by a young man at age 17. In this piece, "housekeeper" takes on a double meaning, revealing both the market and domestic oppression of women.

HOUSEKEEPER

My mom's a housekeeper,
a house persona.
More likely

She works for them,
Keeping their house in tip-top,
while ours is crumbling.

Works for the men.
I hate those shitheads.
And in us she sees the men
The men we become.
The rage on us.

She puts her rage on us,
and age on us.
Hell comes with her.
If one drop of . . .
And the world comes down

My mom's a housekeeper,
Eats, sleeps
And then beats us.
—Gerald Dussap

As a second-generation immigrant from Haiti, Gerald sees inside the lives of women before and after immigration. "Housekeeper," he told me, "is a true story; it comes from the people who surround me. It's a reflection of the lives of women who reared me and it's also a play on the situation that brings them to the United States. In terms of my personal relation to the poem, I never suffered from the violence, but it seems like a lot of Afro-Caribbean women face these situations." Countless Afro-Caribbean women, women who reared my students, were trapped in a "fluid, malleable, secondary labor market by virtue of [their] skin color and their relative lack of appropriate skills" (Limón, 1994, p. 106). Structural changes in the local economy eliminated the possibility of the stable working-class niche occupied by older immigrant groups. When possible, West Indian women in the area moved into low-wage categories such as nursing aides, child-care and private household workers, workers in clerical sales and light manufacturing. Jhoy's mother found a job as a home-care attendant after immigrating from St. Kitts in the early 1990s. Younger West Indian women, students at UHS, brought their nursing aid uniforms to school. After class, they took one or two buses across Brooklyn to hospitals or homes for the aged. Men held jobs in security (ironically, the surveillance industry supports the same population it contains), health services, and the taxi industry (Torres, 1995, p. 122). My students attended high school, wrote poetry, and began their adult lives at a time when New York was increasingly becoming an economically bipolar city (See Table 2.1).

By 1991, deindustrialization had caused extensive job loss, which deepened postwar polarization. Throughout the 1980s and 1990s, the concentration of financial, corporate, and legal services in New York has provided employment to a prosperous layer of highly educated and highly specialized employees serving the dynamic sector of New York's economy. Contrary to the trend in the nation as a whole, real wages actually increased in New York between 1980 and 1995 (Angelo, 1995). However, at the lower pole of the labor market, the shift from a manufacturing to a service economy has meant absolute and relative income decline for the workers of the city. The result is the emergence of a two-tier economy in which a highly paid labor force engaged in financial, corporate, and legal transactions, coexists with low-pay employment in the services. The labor forces of these two different tiers are geographically segregated.

CONTEXTUALIZING A THROW-AWAY SOCIETY

Following city-wide industry patterns, the number of community residents in Crown Heights working as professionals rose. The growth of the profes-

Table 2.1. Labor Force Characteristics, 1990: Brooklyn Community District 9 and Manhattan's Community District 8 (Upper East Side)

	Brooklyn Community District 9	Manhattan Community District 8 (Upper East Side)
Males 16 Years & Over		
In the Labor Force	71%	82%
Not in the Labor Force*	29%	17%
Employed	87%	96%
Unemployed	13%	4%
Females 16 Years & Over		
In the Labor Force	64%	67%
Not in the Labor Force*	36%	33%
Employed	91%	96%
Unemployed	8%	4%
Labor Force Composition		
Male	46%	48%
Female	54%	52%

*Discouraged workers who have been unemployed for years appear in this category, along with children, the elderly, the disabled, and prisoners.

Source: New York City Department of City Planning, *Socioeconomic Profiles: a Portrait of New York City's Community Districts From the 1980 & 1990 Censuses of Population and Housing.* New York: Department of City Planning, March 1993, pp. 174–179, 280–285.

sional and managerial sector was accompanied by an expansion of the informal economy, duplicating within the neighborhood the bipolar employment structure that characterizes the city at large. Informal economies in Crown Heights employ immigrants, high school drop-outs, or underskilled workers, complementing the low-pay service sector as a source of employment and playing an integral role both in the local economy of Crown Heights and in the borough of Brooklyn overall (Ford Foundation, 1993, p. 19). "Dollar vans," for example, transport people for less money than metropolitan buses and subways. The vans run in Black and Latino neighborhoods where mass transit is sporadic, cutting transportation time by hours. UHS students used them frequently. "They come more often and stop in convenient places," they would say.

Some social scientists question the extent of the informal economy and argue that the larger problem, and the one that academics should document, is the proliferation of low-paying jobs in the formal economy (Waldinger & Lapp, 1993, pp. 6–29). Others highlight the sweated trades, a convergence between industrial and Third World labor systems. By acknowledging that an informal economy exists in Central Brooklyn, I do not mean to divert attention away from the low-paying, dead-end jobs that exhausted some of my students, nor do I want to deny the realities of child labor intrinsic to any informal economy; children sold clothes, toys, and hairpieces on the streets of Brooklyn—and many had sold food on the streets of their "home" countries.

Tsahay's memory of Jamaica, of home, of childhood, included, for example, her work as a fish girl:

THE FISH GIRL

There is a girl who stands on the Sea Shore and sells
fish every day.
Her name is Tsahay.
She is only 12 years old. She gets up every day to sell
fish to carry home money to help her mother and six
sisters and brothers. Where she sells the fish she has a
boat, a scaler and a bottle.
She has to stand there all day in the sun until it is
time to go home.

By ninth grade, work experience seeped into student writing. At age 12, Tsahay worked in an informal economy in Jamaica. By age 16, she was working in New York. Countless Brooklyn teenagers stood in markets, under church steeples, because their families faced unemployment and racial discrimination. For these families, marketing in an informal economy was a survival strategy.

Shifting employment trends occurred between 1975 and 1995 (Torres, 1995, p. 35), during a period when the immigrant population of Crown Heights increased dramatically. Forty-five percent of the population in the neighborhood where UHS is located is foreign born, and a majority of these immigrants come from the Caribbean. Between 1982 and 1989, 206,970 people from the non-Hispanic Caribbean immigrated to New York: 72,343 Jamaicans, 53,638 Guyanese, 40,819 Haitians, 20,681 from the Eastern Caribbean, and 13,516 from Trinidad and Tobago (New York City Department of City Planning, 1992, pp. 29, 32). Many of the newcomers settled in Central Brooklyn. Even though the pace of immigration into Crown Heights declined slightly in the first half of the 1990s, the stable communities formed by Caribbean immigrants continued to attract people from essentially the same home countries. Jhoy's family, for example, emigrated from St. Kitts in 1992: "We initially came for a vacation, but one of my aunts talked us into staying." Her aunts had settled in Crown Heights a decade earlier, and in 1992 they made it easier for their relatives to stay in Brooklyn. When Jhoy immigrated with her mother and an older sister, she and her mom moved in with one aunt, and her sister moved in with another. Tanzania's family had immigrated earlier, escaping François Duvalier's autocracy. Her grandmother left Haiti with small children, fearful of the government that held her husband in a military prison.

Living in a Black neighborhood, Jhoy, Tanzania, and their families suffered the same systemic racism as African Americans: failing schools, public and private disinvestments, and a declining tax base. Many studies on so-called "ethnic queues" have confirmed that non-Black immigrants tend to surpass African Americans in levels of income in the second generation. After interviewing West Indian students in two Central Brooklyn high schools, sociologist Mary Waters documented how structural and interpersonal racism caused second-generation immigrants to identify with African Americans and relinquish the cultural beliefs of their families. Specifically, she claims that they began to question the efficacy of education and upward mobility in the face of substandard education and workplace discrimination. "Rightful anger, correct diagnoses of blocked mobility, and prudent protection of one's inner core from these assaults gives rise to cultural and psychological responses that are best described as disinvestment and oppositional identities" (Waters, 1999, p. 335). Unlike previous generations of immigrants, whose cultural assimilation often meant upward mobility, second-generation West Indians will likely face stagnating standards of living or intergenerational downward mobility (Waters, 1999).

HYPERSEGREGATION AND PUBLIC DISINVESTMENT

Students who attended UHS were subject to the historical problems of racism and segregation that characterize the United States. Both the school and the neighborhood that surrounds it reflect the new reality of hypersegregation described by Douglas Massey and Nancy Denton in *American Apartheid: Segregation and the Making of the Underclass* (1993). Contrary to what many Americans believe, the cities of the United States have become steadily more, not less, segregated. Massey and Denton deploy an arsenal of statistics and statistical techniques to show unequivocally that from the times of the U. S. Civil War to the present, despite the gains of the Civil Rights movement, American cities have become increasingly more segregated. New York City is one of the most segregated in the country (Schuman & Sclar, 1998). Segregation was artificially produced in Crown Heights after block-busting—"the practice of inducing panic sales of white homes" (Toscano, 1971, p. 15)—altered the area's racial and economic makeup in the 1960s. This trend was replicated across the United States. Researchers now argue, and data from the 2000 Census concludes, that racial segregation for Blacks is unlike that for any other ethnic or immigrant group, and that more than any other group, Blacks are subject to external segregating forces such as violence and restrictive covenants (Waters, 1999; Scott, 2001c).

Increasing residential segregation in American cities has been accompanied by increasing educational segregation. In 3 years of research at UHS, I did not see a single White student in a population of 2,500. The White children of households in a neighborhood 5 blocks from the school did not attend Urban High School.

In contrast to the South of the United States, where federal government intervention has reduced historical patterns of segregation, public school segregation has increased in the large cities of the North, Midwest, and West. Dr. Gary Orfield of the Harvard Graduate School of Education has pioneered the research on resegregation, showing that the public schools in the North are more segregated than public schools in the South (Applebome, 1997; Glass, Orfield, Reardon, & Schley, 1994; Orfield, 1995). Orfield's recent study, "Schools More Separate: Consequences of a Decade of Resegregation" (2001), indicates that schools became increasingly segregated in the 1990s. By analyzing the 2000 census data, Orfield and a team of Harvard researchers found that 70% of Black children attended predominantly black schools, up from 66% in 1991–1992. The report distinguishes between schools attended by White and minority children, claiming the average Black or Latino child is more likely go to a high-poverty school where students are transient and teachers are less likely to be licensed in their subject areas. In New York City, rezoning—changing the neighborhoods from which a school draws its students—helped create "racially isolated" schools.

Immigration further taxed New York City's segregated schools in the 1980s and 1990s, when the class distribution of the West Indians entering the United States changed to include the poor and the working class. Rezoning and the newer immigration trend contained a population that desperately needed remedial skills. The principal of UHS once told me that the immigrants coming from Panama, teens whose grandparents had emigrated from Jamaica to work on the canal, were illiterate in both Spanish and English.

Of course, education in the Caribbean varies enormously according to country, and the educational backgrounds of newly arrived teenagers have reflected that variation. While tutoring at UHS, I saw Panamanians struggle with basic literacy. Jamaicans from Kingston and Trinidadians from Port of Spain, on the other hand, were often better educated than the African American teens who attended segregated public schools in New York City. As in the United States, education in these countries reflects class origins. In a response to an article in the *New York Times*, "Caribbean Pupils' English Seems Barrier, Not Bridge" (Sontag, 1992), one ninth-grade student from Trinidad wrote

> There is a tremendous gap between the upper and lower classes in Trinidad. On the lower class scale, some students can't go to school because they can't afford it and they've dropped out to help the family survive economically. Those who can go to school to educate themselves in order to advance, so they can migrate to a country, such as America, where limitless opportunities abound.

Seema, the author, was annoyed by the *Times* article and sought to distinguish the variety of educational experiences in her country. Ironically, and in contrast to her belief that limitless opportunities abound in the United States, her prose (its linear development) was better than many of the American-born students I had tutored—students who had been educated in Brooklyn. Prior schooling helped determine academic success. The year that Nikki graduated from UHS, for example, the valedictorian was Jamaican, and he was headed for an elite, 4-year college.

The students attending UHS and other "racially isolated" high schools resented the deterioration and material poverty in their schools. In 1990, at a gathering of educators, I heard Roger Greene, a Brooklyn assemblyman, tell the following story:

> When Mandela visited Boys and Girls High School, he described the schools in South African townships as inferior. He said classes were overcrowded, schools needed math teachers, and buildings were falling down. Five minutes into the description, the teens who were listening responded in unison: Here too. "Teachers cannot give every child a book." Here too. "Few students graduate." Here too.[1]

The year I began tutoring at UHS, the schools in the neighborhood were the fourth most overcrowded in New York City, with many of the elementary schools operating at over 100% capacity (Crown Heights Coalition, 1992, pp. 28–36). According to a report initiated by the borough president's office, the youth services in Crown Heights, during the time of my research, were grossly inadequate: "The level of service is so low that for every 2,300 youths there is only one youth service provider" (Crown Heights Coalition, 1992, p. 36). In a 4-year financial plan released in 1995, New York City mayor Rudolph Giuliani called for the elimination of nearly all youth serv-ices. Among the programs cut was Street Outreach, "which trained workers to go into neighborhoods to spread the word about youth programs and recruit for anti-violence programs" (Mitchell, 1995, p. B5).

As public investment decreased, assault weapons flooded urban markets, making Harvey's conception of a throw-away society a deadly reality. In 1992, the leading cause of death for New York City's 15–24-year-olds was homicide (Citizens Committee for Children of New York, 1995, p. 25). Sullivan and Miller are careful to point out that this statistic does not mean that more teens became violent. "Lethality, not incidence or precedence, is the principal vec-tor of change in adolescent violence" (Sullivan & Miller, 1999, 262–263). Although the number of teens committing crime never rose, the rate of ado-lescent homicide from the mid-1980s through the early 1990s was unprece-dented. Jamie (a 15-year-old) puts a face on the overwhelming loss:

> JAMIE: You know what, Jennifer, I heard that a boy from UHS died.
> JENNIFER: Who?
> JAMIE: A Dominican, he hung out on the second floor where the Dominicans hang out.
> JENNIFER: What happened?
> JAMIE: He got stabbed several times but a wound to the head killed him. His friends cried. Nineteen-year-old boys—I'd never seen older boys cry. There ain't nothing sadder than that. (June 1993)

Her voice is empathic. She has seen boys cry, carries the image with her, articulating it repeatedly. This visualization allows her to imagine the pain that accompanies death and "there ain't nothing sadder than that."

During the 2 years I tutored at UHS, I met young people who desper-ately tried to move away from crime-ridden projects. One social worker working with teen mothers told me: "One of my parents applied to move to another housing unit because her current building is so dangerous. Drug dealers knock on her door at all hours of the night. She sent letters from psychologists to public housing authorities indicating that violence in the building had a negative impact on her two-year-old. But housing officials eventually rejected this woman's application. They said there were others with greater needs." Images of the projects appeared in student poetry. The class poem cited in Chapter 1 begins:

I see myself in the projects.
People are fighting. They
look busted. I hear babies crying.
I see a lot of welfare stores.
Cops on the corner.
"Fuck you" "Bullshit"
"Bitch" "You Punk" "Slut"
They fight with automatic weapons,
a razor, a machete. They drink malt liquor.
Smoking reefers. Lots of graffiti on the wall.

Images of violence seeped into Nikki's dreams. Months after she witnessed a shooting in a local skating rink, she still had nightmares. When I asked her if anyone had been hurt, she looked at me incredulously. She replied, "I got trampled on, and someone got shot in the arm. One guy got shot in the face." After the shooting, she seemed to construct a shield that protected her from feeling pain but prevented them from entering another's mind. While behind that shield, Nikki cannot depend on friends because "you know they are going to be gone soon."

JENNIFER: Alright. In your learning at UHS have you come across an idea that made you see things differently?
NIKKI: No. Well this school makes you know that you don't have any friends.
JENNIFER: You don't?
NIKKI: You have to know you have to live on your own. You can't depend on them because you know they are going to be gone soon. Like they can be here once and the next thing you know they're gone.
JENNIFER: Why do they come and go so often?
NIKKI: They either don't get along with somebody or they gotta move away somewhere or something happens like they got

killed or something. One way or another they leave because
they don't have a choice. (Interview with Nikki, November
1993)

In this context, Nikki's unwillingness to become close to others is intricately connected to her perception that social life shifts too suddenly to be trustworthy. Transience disallows any sense of belonging. Consequently, "you must live on your own." For those who "move away," alienation takes on a newer meaning: powerlessness, or a feeling that you are incapable of affecting your own fate. "Friends" leave because they are devoid of agency, "because they don't have a choice." Thus the absence of permanence was often devastating, for it fostered a state of alienation, an estrangement from others.

Law enforcement's fear of violence has increased racial profiling in Black neighborhoods, a practice that presumes criminality, along with aggressive stop-and-frisk policies. Tanzania, Nikki, and Nessa often saw police behavior as erratic and deadly. In a quiet voice that was barely discernible, Nessa once told me:

NESSA: I don't take those dollar vans no more. I was in one of
them when the police pulled us over, drew their guns, and told
us to get out. They kept their guns drawn as we left the van.
JENNIFER: Why did they draw their guns?
TANZANIA: Because they're trigger happy.
NESSA: Just look at the Diallo case. Forty-one bullets, my god.
(December 27, 1999)

Nikki was equally suspicious: "They are everywhere; they are all over my neighborhood, and they look for trouble. I saw cops frisk kids when all they were doing was hanging out on my block playing dominoes." The rape and torture of Abner Louima, a Haitian immigrant, by a New York City police officer, occurred in a precinct near UHS. That case reveals another dimension of complete discard.

Profiling, dwindling public services, increasing racial segregation, substandard schools, and violence marginalized many of the area's residents, effectively reducing the life chances of its children. Andre, one of Hermine's students, powerfully sums ups the spiritual consequences of marginalization in "I Had Lost My Voice." In the following passage, he does not preserve people and places, but records his psychic destruction in the Van Dyke Projects.

I had lost my voice from yelling at this kid who was an asshole. I yelled at him while we were walking up the staircase. I wanted to shoot him but I couldn't. Why couldn't I? Was it my conscience that stopped me? But naw, it couldn't be, because I don't have one. He looked like he didn't know anything, like he didn't have a clue, that I had to murder him because I was paid to. Next after the yelling all you heard was a gunshot and a person falling. Someone's father stuck his head out the door and I shot him too. I didn't think he would believe me if I claimed self-defense, so I murdered the bastard and laid him to rest. I heard a scream, someone shouted for help, so I ran down the stairs. On my way out of the building, someone was eyeing me, I was going to shoot him too, but I just ran and let it be. I flew like a bird out of Van Dyke Projects, because I wasn't about to get caught. That night all I could hear was the scream from that apartment. That's when I swore I'd never do a hit unless I was in danger. So now I carry a gun only for protection, with no intention to hurt nobody. Maybe one day I will be out of danger, but only when someone puts me out of my misery. Then neither my body nor my mind will feel pain and my tortured soul will no longer be left wandering.

No agent accompanies the first gunshot; there is no triggerman. Personal responsibility gets erased, and we enter a world devoid of feeling. Entry into this void begins with a loss of voice, the mark of persona or personhood. The latter half of the text is replete with what Fredric Jameson (1984) calls the anxiety of an earlier age. Alienation, a sense of some lost agency and purpose, never quite gives way to an inability to conceive agency. The appearance of "I" indicates a subject, but, even more hauntingly, it shows the writer's ability to hear terror externalized, the scream. Locked within an individual consciousness, he is never detached from feeling, but plagued by anxiety, guilt, isolation, and terror. The last sentence ["Then neither my body nor my mind will feel pain, and my tortured soul will no longer be left wandering"], with its sense of loss and desperation, captures an individual who is internally divided and completely alone.

Throughout her life, Nessa has lost people she loves. She wrote the poem "Subbie" after her uncle died. She came to the tutoring room sad and preoccupied, and when I asked her what was wrong, she showed me the poem. In it, she talks to her aunt Subbie, and through a dialogue she acknowledges her strength and her will to survive. The turn-taking, conversational structure affirms Nessa's willingness to make people whole, and ultimately, celebrates relationship.

Subbie, what's happening to me?
I think I'm falling apart.
No, You're just going through a rough time now
with your mother dying,
grandfather, grandmother, uncle.
You are known to be a strong, willing person
to get behind your troubles.
Subbie you're right I'm strong
and I will put this behind me.
Because that's what they would want,
I think it is best for me too.
Good for you Nessa.
Because I'm here
and I will take the place of all of them
and love you even more NOW.
—Nessa, age 16

When Nessa wrote "Subbie," George H. Bush was president; he had succeeded 8 years of Reaganomics, a period characterized by the slow erosion of social programs and the rise of corporate greed. In a gripping book that chronicles the soul of hip-hop, Nelson George writes, "The go-go capitalism of Reagan's America flowed down to the streets stripped of its jingoistic patriotism and fake piety. The unfettered free market of crack generated millions and stoked a voracious appetite for 'goods,' and not good" (1998, p. 41). George goes on to note that the materialism of the 1980s replaced spirituality and "an appreciation of life's intangible pleasures took a beating in places where children became disposable and sex was commodified" (p. 41). Nessa's poem is testament to the intangible pleasures that keep her alive; it is an emotionally laden tribute to Subbie. Nessa has been orphaned and she is surrounded by drug addiction, but she is not one of the children in Kashan's poem, for she is not disposable. And she will not become disposable, because Subbie takes the place of her mother, "of all of them," and loves her, now.

IMAGES OF PERMANENCE

City geography reinforces, and to a certain extent allows, local business. New York's immigrant groups, its ethnic queues, have created "semiautonomous village communities" (Ross, 2002, p. 124). Newcomers settle in enclaves, and even long-term residents refer to ethnic neighborhoods when describing where they live. Informal business, specifically markets, has, in turn, helped characterize local life. Andrew Ross (2002) quotes a WPA guide to New York in order to describe the markets of the city's old Syrian quarter: "[A]lthough the fez has given way to the snap-brim, and the narghile has been abandoned for cigarettes, the coffee houses and the tobacco and confectionery shops of the Levantines still remain" (p. 123). The Syrian quarter was undercut by the expansion of the financial district in the 1920s and ultimately cleared for the construction of the World Trade Center. Despite urban renewal and slum clearance, the tenacity of local life (and local markets) has been evident throughout the city's history and remains evident in neighborhoods claimed by its newest immigrants—Sunset Park has become Brooklyn's Chinatown, southern Brooklyn sprouts Russian villages, and Flatbush is a Caribbean, and increasingly an African, oasis.

Gerald wrote "Merchants" after watching Senegalese vendors on the streets of Brooklyn. The poem beautifully details the sounds of markets from DeKar to New York.

> They lay their merchandise
> on streets, and embalming the air with
> the smells of eggs,
> fresh vegetables.
> When by misfortune your feet
> step on any of their squash
> mille pardons you must utter for
> if not curses from the
> finest gypsies will lay upon your head.
>
> Walking along,
> each corner, different cries overheard.
> And behind all that there are
> always rooster fights, bet on the
> best rooster and make a thousand purse
> made of all sorts of animals' hide, shoes
> lay on the sidewalk like dead fish
> after a tornado. Gold chains to satisfy
> a pirate's thirst
>
> And each merchant go on singing the
> same litany.
> —Gerald Dussap

The social interaction depicted in these scenes, the cockfights, the curses, the merchant's litany, are all evidence that the informal economy is not simply a legalistic definition, but an expression of cultural and social identity. New York City politicians have complained about the exotic mélange. Ed Koch, the city's former mayor, said, "I believe it ruins the ambiance." Referring to the vendors in downtown Brooklyn, he continued, "This is not supposed to look like a souk" (Hemphill & Whitaker, 1988, pp. 3, 31). As Harvey suggests, the Caribbean markets of New York represent survival strategies for the unemployed and those who are discriminated against, yet their impact on local neighborhoods, and the city itself, amounts to more than individual survival. Tanzania described her mother's decision to market as a desire for freedom and then mentioned her popularity with customers, her ability to be witty, and her willingness to swap stories with other vendors: "My mother wanted to feel her own independence and she wanted an immediate connection to people; her customers liked her; she was funny. And she looked so alive in the market, so alive."

Marketing consecrates a connection to place. It generates sites of social interaction that depend on "diversity, intricacy, and the capacity to handle the unexpected in controlled but creative ways" (Harvey, 1989, p. 73). The merchants of central Brooklyn grab what they can to make a living. They respond to regularity, routine, and complete spontaneity, engaging tedium and chaos in an attempt to establish order. By moving the personal and individual into a very public realm, market strategies are subject to constant revision. Tanzania writes:

> My mother can set a trend in the neighborhood. She'll get someone who is well known, around my block, to buy her glasses. Then others will ask, "And where did you buy these?" Or I will wear my silver rings, when I help my mother sell jewelry. Girls talk to me when I do. They always notice the rings.

Tanzania's mother invigorates public space by setting a trend. She makes a place for herself in a public arena, puts herself in the center of that arena, and, finally, devises a means to create and maintain social interaction. Both women engage their neighbors, constructing strategies to sell goods. Tanzie subsequently captures that activity in a narrative. The image of marketing that remains with her signals a control that seems to resurface in her poem "I Am Luna," in which she transforms herself into the moon and determines "just how much of me I'd want everyone to see."

The decline of industry, relatively high unemployment in city centers, the privatization of collective needs, and an unyielding cultural emphasis on superficiality have taken a toll on the people of Crown Heights. As one student put it: "without a label, you're nothing." This emphasis on labels, a culture of the image engendered by consumerism, exists alongside a consecration of memory that often connects newly arrived immigrants to their home countries. The market on Flatbush Avenue endures, as do parodies such as *Scandals, Lies and a Visa*. Seen against an abandoned landscape littered with crack vials, the comedy claims collective existence, protecting the people of Crown Heights against reduction or disappearance. The market, moreover, is an interesting contrast to capital flight or uselessness; despite family labor and ultimate exploitation, it appears to run on its own steam, oblivious to the remnants of tragedy that are strewn nearby. I have come to read it as a reminder of human potential.

The square outside Brooklyn's oldest church is a place where people encounter each other, chat, mingle, and then go home. The women who market here have deepened a neighborhood's connection to place; they have ensured human interaction and etched their own permanence into New York City. Their livelihoods and memories enable them to resist the systematic acceptance of a throw-away society. Under a white steeple, Haitian women remind us that city space is inexhaustible, it "folds over on itself in so many [cultural] layers and relationships" (Young, 1990, p. 24). Tanzania writes:

> I never ask my grandmother about her life, but when she tells stories, I listen. [She puts her hands on the table and thrusts her body forward to imitate anticipation.] My grandmother left Haiti after my grandfather was imprisoned by the government. Afraid someone would come after her, hurt her, hurt her family, she moved to Brooklyn with her daughters. She did not know English. She raised my aunt and my mother by working two jobs. [She catches my eye and her voice softens.] You know, my grandmother was a beautiful woman, physically beautiful.

Tanzania is a physically beautiful woman, as well. She carries her grandmother with her—circulating the old woman's story like a silver ring. That story transcends individual survival; it crosses generations to form a connective tissue that binds the listener to people, places, and received ways of doing and being. Stories of women who have crossed an ocean to raise their daughters, and the market strategies of central Brooklyn residents, are reflected in images of possibility at UHS.

> I pull the waves at my own will
> and push them away when I'm through

I have control
More control than the sun.
(From "I Am Luna," Tanzania)

In "Letter to a Young Writer," written days after the attack on the World Trade Center, Susan Mitchell reflected on the role of the poet in the midst of vast destruction. She reminds us that the Romans had three terms for poet—"prophet," "writer of songs," and "conditor"—someone who built store-rooms for valuables (Mitchell, 2001, p. 27). Nessa and Tanzania built store-rooms. They used language to preserve loved ones, emotional ties, and images of themselves. Poetic language, like the storytelling that cemented a market, bound the poet (or speaker) to her audience; it was the connective tissue, the cord that ran between I and you in "Subbie." It saved the writer's perception of self—her strength and her willingness *to get behind her troubles*—and it allowed her to share those perceptions with others.[2] Nessa and Tanzania held onto the lives of generations, and then held them up to their readers. By doing so, they wrote against the concept of a throw-away society, and the psychic destruction that accompanies marginalization.

NOTES

1. This story was told in the *New York Times* as follows: "The state of education in our country is very bad indeed," Mr. Mandela said. "The education is inferior for blacks." He seemed to be drawing a contrast between conditions in his home country and those he perceived here, but his audience took it another way. "It's the same here," yelled a man. "Our education is not controlled by our people but by whites," Mr. Mandela went on. A chant rolled from the crowd: "Same here, same here" (*New York Times*, June 29, 1990, late ed.; sec. A; p. 14, col. 3. Also see *New York Newsday*, June 21, 1990, p. 4.)

2. Muriel Rukeyser also defined poetry as "a saving thing": "I do believe that the forces in our wish to share something of experience by turning it into something and giving it to somebody: that is poetry. That is some kind of saving thing, and as far as my life is concerned, poetry has saved me again and again" (Rukeyser, 1994, p. 283).

CHAPTER 3

Drag Me to the Asylum

I'm scared of the thing around
They're going to get me.
I'm scared of what people say
about me. They don't like me.
Why? because I'm different
from them. I come from a poor
family. Clothes I have to wear
everyday holes in my sneakers.
I'm scared of what's going to
happen to me.
—Nessa, age 16

In 1991, when I began tutoring in Urban High School (UHS), weapon searches occurred periodically. Roughly 40 guards would arrive in five or six police vans for what was known as "scan day." The vans lined the school's front entrance, parking along an entire city block. By the time my tutoring assignment ended in 1993, the New York City Board of Education had installed weapon-scanning metal detectors in 41 schools, and scanning became systematic at Urban High School. This act was a direct reaction to the shooting deaths of two students at another Brooklyn high school on February 26, 1992.

Horrified by the loss of life, politicians and educators expanded high-tech weapons searches by appealing to the public's concern for safety. "The city cannot do business as usual," said Sandra Feldman, president of the teachers union; "we're losing our kids" (Berger, 1992, p. B4). Under mounting pressure from civic leaders to combat a "clear and present life threatening danger," mayor David Dinkins promised money for tighter security (Steinberg, 1992, p. A1). From the pulpit of a Brooklyn Baptist church, he pledged 28 million dollars to ensure safety in the city's most dangerous public schools, and then evoked the memory of Martin Luther King, Jr.: "We did

57

not let so many members of one generation die for freedom, only to watch a new generation die for a pair of sneakers or a gold chain or a leather jacket" (Steinberg, 1992, p. A1). His efforts were applauded by the Board of Education. In 1994, school chancellor Ramón Cortines called for the city to further bolster school security after yet another shooting had occurred in a school corridor (Dillon, 1994, p. B3). Meanwhile, political rhetoric continued to accompany parental fear and the escalation of security. After touring Sheepshead Bay High School, Dinkins's successor, Rudolph Giuliani, told reporters, "A school is a sacred place" (Sexton, 1994, p. A27). That year the number of metal detectors in schools grew to 47 (Devine, 1996, p. 23), and Giuliani repeatedly asked the New York City Board of Education to approve a permanent police presence.

Security guards had entered schools much earlier, however; 200 first appeared in 1969 (Dillon, 1993a). By 1995, there were over 3,000 uniformed "safety officers" in New York City public schools, "a force bigger than that of the entire Boston Police Department" (Devine, 1995, p. 172). Dismissing their effectiveness, Giuliani continued to pressure the schools' chancellor and its board members to relinquish control over security, essentially demanding a police takeover: "I think parents and teachers would feel far safer if this were in the hands of the N.Y.P.D" (Newman, 1995, p. B4). The Board of Education responded by placing highly sensitive metal detectors in 34 high schools. The detectors were so powerful that students had to take their belts off to move through school entrances. In one South Bronx school, teens renamed the hallway outside the cafeteria "Belt Alley" (Toy, 1995, p. B3).

As a student enters the front door at UHS, she inserts an identification card into an "access machine." It responds, "Good morning." It indicates whether she has arrived early or late. It displays the time. If she has committed a violation, a red light blinks on. The light is followed by a code that marks the nature of her offense. A "D" means a trip to the dean's office, an "S" signals current suspension. If the student has not been immunized, "N" sends her to the nurse's office. A yellow light signals her birthday. Once past the machine, the student places her bookbag through an x-ray conveyor belt. She may then be asked to spread her legs and stretch her hands out in front of her so a security guard can wave a portable metal detector over her body. Inside the building, metal locks, tracking machines (guard-operated, computerized machines that record attendance), and the continuous presence of uniformed guards curtail student movement.

FROM TRAINING TO CONTAINMENT

Through the first half of the 20th century, students were assessed according to how they performed on tests, and they passed through a succession of subjects that progressed according to increasing difficulty. Goaded by criticism, educators sought to make growing public school systems more efficient by measuring skill development or "products" (Callahan, 1962; Oakes, 1985). Speed became synonymous with educational success. Through regimentation, surveillance, and the assessment of large numbers of students, schools functioned like factories. They also prepared teens for entry into the labor force. The ideological and economic roles of these schools were thus interconnected. Regimentation, the movement of student bodies, and individual assessment roughly reproduced a hierarchical labor force that was stratified along racial, class, and gendered lines (Apple & Weis, 1983, p. 5). Stratification occurred, in part, as different groups were taught distinct skills, knowledge, and values. White girls in working-class Brooklyn neighborhoods learned to sew in the 1930s and 1940s, while structural and interpersonal racism prevented Black girls from entering select New York City vocational schools.

As security became a primary concern at UHS, the school's administration and the New York City Board of Education altered traditional scholastic routines and the school's physical design. Attempts to measure individual progress, collect homework, record lateness, and curb absenteeism continue despite the school's emphasis on security, but they have been subordinated to exercises intended to contain teenagers and curtail violence. The mixture of diverse institutional practices visible at UHS indicates paradoxical functions: to educate, to prepare students for their participation in social life, and to hold them back or enclose them.

The principles of industry—speed, efficiency, continuity, a detailed partitioning of time, the organization of teachers' work into concrete goals, the belief that knowledge is a product, and the perception that educational gains, or products, can be measured—still organize the day-to-day interactions of teachers, students, and administrators in high schools like UHS, but "the factory" has become an increasingly inadequate description of these schools. In fact, UHS often functions as a holding tank, defined as much by its locked doors as by its lack of resources. This shift toward containment was not planned. Fearful of potential violence, politicians and school administrators have prioritized security, creating an amalgam of institutional models for large, public high schools. The layers of this amalgamation shift with public concerns. During the early 1990s, for example, the New York City Board of Education responded to a widespread fear of student violence by installing metal detectors in 41 schools. By 1995, the board employed over 3,000 security guards. These responses began to reshape the purpose of inner-city schools: the role of the institution became increasingly negative. High schools attempted to curtail violence; they attempted to arrest it. The current stress on standards as a way to produce skills has shifted institutional priorities once again. In Foucauldian terms, UHS, like other schools in working-class Black neighborhoods, has begun to function a little more like a panopticon (designed to increase individual utility) and a little less like an enclosed institution (designed to contain "useless" or "dangerous" populations).

The layers of routines and architectural designs raise questions regarding the relationship between school and society: specifically, what is the connection between amalgamation and marginalization? Between amalgamation and racial stratification? This chapter answers how a particular conceptual order became prevalent in one high school. It then looks at how student poetry reflected and interrupted that order.

"WE NEED MORE SECURITY"

Urban High School began in 1923 as Girls Commercial High. During the 1940s and 1950s, Italian and Jewish girls learned to sew, design clothes, and write for the school newspaper. Vocational and academic boundaries undoubtedly merged for these students, but looking at old newspaper photographs, I see women who are prepared to work. In one picture, a young woman, identified as a staff member of the school newspaper, looks directly at the machinery of a printing press. Below her, a caption reads "The Real Thing." In another photo, six women smile and look off to the side. Each models a costume that she has designed and sewn herself. Names are listed underneath the photo, five names followed by "the first prize winner of the show, Aspasia Costas"—six women judged, ranked, and rewarded. In another image, a woman sits in front of a typewriter and is labeled according to vocation, a "Commercial High reporter." Like the students who have sewn marketable objects, she has been trained to produce.

In 1948, Loeser's Department Store, the New York City Board of Education, and the home economics department at UHS sponsored a consumer-retailer project for students who could design their own dresses (Eagle

Staff Photo, 1948, p. 3). Thirty-seven years later, the Pepsi-Cola Bottling Company adopted the high school under the Join-a-School program. As part of the program, Pepsi established a scholar of the month award for improved academic performance; they offered cash for good grades (McCallister, 1985, p. K8). In 1985 ranking was still profitable, and it was linked to occupational training. One representative from Pepsi stated, "The bottom line is that we all have a stake in the city's public schools. . . . They are training our future work force" (McCallister, 1985, p. K8). The speaker concedes that schools produce labor and technical know-how; an unspoken assumption is that they also produce consumerism. However, by 1985 Urban High School's administration and its teachers had begun to emphasize containment over training. In 1977, 2 years after the school went coed and approximately a decade after the student population became primarily Black, police were entering UHS to question teenagers and, at times, to arrest them (Kappstatter, 1977). Teachers were demanding permanent security guards and the United Federation of Teachers was threatening job actions to protest what it perceived as an administrative failure to respond to school violence. The shifting sentiment was summed up by one of the school's union reps: "We need more security guards. The hell with the budget, the hell with everything else" (cochairman, school chapter, United Federation of Teachers, quoted in Kappstatter, 1977, p. K4). The possibility of violence would alter Board of Education priorities over the next 20 years.

Consequently, academic assessment, "the rank attributed to each pupil at the end of each task" (Bracken, 1992, p. 234), is no longer the only means of sorting a student population. Teens are now harmless or dangerous. The focus on security has occurred alongside large-scale systemic failure. As of 2001, only half of New York City high school students were graduating in 4 years; that number has been relatively the same for a decade (Hartocollis, 2001, p. B6). In 1994, 64% of an entire class at UHS failed to graduate on time. At commencement, UHS's principal announced that 100 students would not move on with their class. An additional 150 students disappeared between fall 1991 and spring 1995. Similar statistics exist for other schools that serve immigrant populations that are Black and Latino. While some students may have transferred, the numbers suggest that many are repeating grades—or dropping out. Teens who fail to graduate and live in deindustrialized cities like New York face greater economic marginalization than youth who drop out in cities where there is a factory-based economy, because they have fewer alternatives for mainstream work (Perlmann & Waldinger, 1998).

"Outside" repeatedly surfaced in my notes as a literal and metaphorical reference. Kids are outside school, outside academic supervision, and all too often outside a mainstream labor force. Perceptions of civil servants reflect and reinforce Iris Marion Young's assertion that some groups (the elderly, the poor, single mothers, and, in this case, Black teenagers) are "thrown away" or expelled from useful participation in social life. After encountering a New York City police officer on the steps of UHS, a nervous preservice teacher showed him a list of schools and asked which one she should choose as a site for student teaching; he replied, "Go to a vocational option school; Urban High School is a *waiting station* between junior high school and jail."[1] His metaphor suggests that an entire student population is being prepared to remain outside the workforce and is, essentially, expendable.

"THE CULT OF EFFICIENCY"[2]

City schools have historically confronted fiscally conservative publics, streams of immigrants, and general overcrowding. The volume of children coursing into school buildings at the turn of the 20th century hastened a demand for efficiency; schools began to cram "as much learning as possible into [a single] day" (Bracken, 1992, p. 234). Students were supervised, ranked, and rewarded with an intensity that has disappeared in inner-city high schools. Schooling routines that emphasized promptness and skill development took on increasing importance after Frederick Taylor devised a system to increase labor productivity. It was implemented with a stopwatch and a recording card (Callahan, 1962; Harvey, 1989). With the adoption of Taylorism to education, observation and individual placement became locked within a grid. Students were assessed according to their academic abilities and then sorted into ranks. Time and motion became paramount to academic tasks. Bodily movement had to be controlled to ensure maximum productivity (Bracken, 1992; Callahan, 1962; Foucault, 1979; Noguera, 1995). Industry had become a model for education. Its values, specifically its regard for efficiency, translated into educational standards that privileged speed and accuracy. The timelessness and temporary chaos of thinking were subsequently deemphasized or dismissed.

Many manuals published during the early 20th century describe learning in atomistic terms. Students were not depicted as working collectively; work was, in fact, conceived of as an individual, intellectual act that allowed teachers to judge, rank, and mark the students in their classes. Simultaneously, effective teaching was reduced to the teacher's ability to underscore individual differences. It was a didactic interaction that yielded cumulative results:"

> If a class is well taught, that is, if the pupils are stimulated or encouraged
> to work to the limit of their ability, individual differences will appear in
> the work accomplished early in the term, and these differences will
> increase as the work progresses (New York City Board of Education,
> 1922, p. 109).

Measuring individual difference underscores a notion of individualism that is based on possession (Apple, 1983); everyone accumulates a quantity of assessable skills, and their worth is then determined by the skills they possess.

In the United States, school administrators incorporated the principles of Taylorism into instruction as early as 1911. Teachers attempted to teach 150 to 200 students a day during 45- to 60-minute periods. By the 1930s, superintendents took steps to increase the size of secondary classes, school buildings, and teaching loads (Callahan, 1962, p. 232). The movement of an increasingly large number of bodies necessitated a means of checking to see whether people were in the right place at the right time. Students were thus tracked according to age and academic ability: "[P]laces [were] assigned for all pupils of all lessons, so that all those attending the same lesson will always occupy the same place" (Foucault, 1979, p. 147). We see the same pattern of serial space at Bethlehem Steel, where "every laborer's work was planned out well in advance, and the workmen were all moved from place to place by the clerks with elaborate diagrams or maps of the yard before them, very much as chessmen on a chessboard"(Callahan, 1962, p. 33).

Moreover, students were thrust into an environment in which every spelling bee, recitation, and timed multiplication exam counted toward promotion. Individualization was increasingly achieved through examination. "Through the use of such instruments, we have not only been made aware of individual differences in our pupils in a more objective way, but we have also been able to measure the extent of such differences" (New York City Board of Education, 1922, p. 115). Educators developed achievement tests in language arts and math. Following the industry's regard for efficiency, they valued speed and accuracy.

The first 25 years of the 20th century were marked by the administration of scientific tests, the expansion of tracking, and the keeping of detailed records on students from IQs to physical history and recreational interests. The "principle underlying such progress was the recognition of individual differences" (Tyack, 1974, p. 182). Despite this emphasis on individualization, African Americans were continually channeled into low-performing classes. In 1923, 25% of all Black children in Cleveland were assigned to special education classes, although an equal number of Black and White children were born with special needs (Tyack, p. 220). Individual African Americans who subverted the system and graduated from college were often barred from white-collar professions (Tyack; Wilder, 2000). Racism thus conflicted with the myth of meritocracy and reinforced a stratified workforce.

However, past discrimination functioned in schools that were often socially productive. Early 20th-century schools in racially stratified America produced a labor force and spread skills and notions of morality. They taught Black girls how to hold their bodies in order to find work as maids (Tyack, 1974, p. 219). UHS, on the other hand, has asked its students to assume a criminal stance as they enter the front door, and the stance has become the school's first assessment of the student body: the first assessment of its guilt. Scanning may help authorities identify dangerous teenagers, but it does not produce anything. Like earlier routines that augmented skill development, it consumes the student's body, specifying where she must position her fingers, arms, and legs, but does not lead to efficiency and speed. Scanning arrests the student; it completely isolates her. We see a fundamental opposition to that which is useful in Tanzania's language; scanning is "*not* good"; it is *not a productive* way to start off school" (See Chapter 4).

The exact relationship between self-expression and constraint is hard to discern. The poetic "I" can originate with the kind of subjection that is negotiated within a cage (or a Goffmanesque asylum), yet writing is an act of appropriation. Through it, teens can replicate entrapment or assert another kind of order within containment. Lakee wrote "The Animal I Am" after Hermine told her to become the animal she resembles. The poem followed a series of creative exercises that required students to imagine a physical transformation. Although she transforms the assignment, Lakee is caught within a fixed perception of herself and others. Metaphor itself contains her, obscuring her multi-dimensional identity: her silent strength, her willingness to write, often and alone, her academic interests—even, and perhaps particularly, her petite female body. We cannot see beyond *the animal*, beyond what she sees, a singular vision, which becomes as real and as binding as that body.

> Actually I'm not really like an animal. But being myself is living wild just like in animals because I'm curious at all times. I don't trust no one. Never liking to be a follower having to get what I want in many different ways even if it involves violence and jumping and ready to attack anyone or anything that's in the way of my path for me and my key to success.

And the animal I'm like is called
Myself!   (I don't compare myself
                              to no one
                              or
                              nothing)

This writer problematizes the animal/human binary that Hermine assumes. She takes on an animal likeness without embodying a particular animal. She boasts about living wild and trusting no one, and thereby subverts the evolutionary ladder that has humans at its pinnacle. Lakee is unwilling to be "a follower," a member of the metaphorical pack. She perceives multiple routes to success, but does not rule out violence. She will attack to succeed. When I asked her why she compared herself to an animal, she replied: "Because my eyes are open at all times."

> JENNIFER: Why do you think you have to be that way?
> LAKEE: Wide eye [3 seconds of silence] . . . Some people just jump
>   at you for nothing. You can be minding your own business
>   and they hit on you, just to get a rep . . . so my eyes are open
>   at all times.
> JENNIFER: Why do you think it's like that?
> LAKEE: Actually I really can't say. People act for different reasons.
>   Some just do to be down or be known.
> JENNIFER: To be known?
> LAKEE: To be popular.
> JENNIFER: That wins popularity?
> LAKEE: To some people it does. Yeah, because some say "you heard
>   about Keisha she did this to that person" and Keisha thinks
>   she's being known.

Her response situates "The Animal I Am" within a world where trust is fragile, if not impossible, and it reflects the school's rationale for containment. Students are not to be trusted. Lakee's animal metaphor and the school's metal detectors are grounded in the reality of student violence, but this reality becomes magnified by past reputations, which has forged a cycle of mistrust.

In other words, school authorities have set up the conditions in which violence and mistrust seem like expected routes to subjecthood. They have normalized a high-tech police response to *all* student behavior. In this context, violence appears inevitable. Listen to one young woman describe how she was searched at the school. As she stands with her arms outstretched, as she takes money out of her pocket, she is conscious of an audience.

> JENNIFER: How are you scanned?
> EVA: You have to open up your coat and stand with your arms out-
> stretched [she stretches her arms]. You have to take money out
> of your pocket, and you might not want everyone to know
> you have money. Strip everything in your pocket.

Now listen back and forth between Eva's description of the search and Lakee's poem and you hear replication.

> You have to open up your coat;
> I don't trust no one
>
> Take money out of your pocket;
> I don't trust no one.

Tone and syntax are eerily similar. Lakee's imagery—the wide-eyed caution, the protective instincts—may not have been initiated by UHS policy, but its emotional resonance parallels that policy and was likely reinforced at the school's front door.

SUBORDINATING ASSESSMENT

Although UHS students were sorted into "harmless" and/or "dangerous" cat-egories on a daily basis, they were never routinely judged and ranked for the academic work they completed. They periodically took state mandated tests, but teachers did not assess them habitually. More pointedly, both standard-ized and individual assessment was often meaningless. I have met young peo-ple who received A's for copying information from a dictionary, and I have watched teachers and administrators give a perfect attendance award to a stu-dent who never showed up for class.

> A story that comes to mind when looking back on last week's
> events stems from my trip to the mini-school—an area set aside for
> students labeled "at risk." I went to talk with Yvonne Saunders, a
> young woman who indicated that she needed help with English.

Unfortunately, I interrupted an awards ceremony. Yvonne would have received an award for perfect attendance, if she had been present. One of the teachers dispensing certificates claimed she had never seen Yvonne. I searched for this student the next day, but to no avail. Another teacher I questioned about the girl's whereabouts confided that Yvonne could not read a word of English "despite the fact that she had been raised in the United States." (Observational notes, September 30, 1991)

Specious awards existed alongside inflated test scores. Fear of state condemnation prompted administrators to "go easy on students." According to one social studies teacher: "Getting students to pass the Regents Comprehensive Tests was the most important aspect of our job; we were told this in no uncertain terms. My chair said that thirty percent of every class should pass the social studies RCT [Regents Competency Test] exam. When I graded exams I was told to go easy on students. My chair said this to me. Other members of my department said it" (Former social studies teacher, March 1997). Rather than measure skill, exams consequently homogenized the student population. Regardless of state pressure, however, few students in the school graduated with New York's esteemed Regents' diploma, an achievement that signified entry into selective colleges. When Nikki graduated in 1995, only 9 teens out of a graduating class of 250 received Regents' diplomas.

Paradoxically, policy decisions often undermined graduation rates. The year Nikki graduated, massive cuts in city spending prompted schools to cut the academic loads of underachieving students. Students who failed courses were given truncated programs; consequently they took fewer credits per semester and remained in school longer than their more academically successful peers. Administrators refer to the decision to cut a student's academic load as a "guidance determination." The practice was widespread in low-income areas. According to Noreen Connell, the executive director of the budget watchdog group Educational Priorities Panel, "High schools serving low-income communities are targeting students for shorter days and, of course, that allows them to decrease their teaching staff" (Taylor, 1995, p. A21).

Young people often blamed the school for not preparing them for life after graduation. When I asked Nikki what the school had failed to provide her, she responded:

NIKKI: A lot of schools they have science fairs. Here they don't try to get you involved in anything. They don't try to tell you

about stuff. The only thing they got you doing is, certain ath-
letics, like basketball. That's all they base their school about.

JENNIFER: Sports?

NIKKI: Yeah, sports. And a lot of these kids ain't getting passed by
no sports.

JENNIFER: Uh-huh.

NIKKI: They are not providing a lot of stuff.

JENNIFER: What would you like them to provide?

NIKKI: Like college course classes.

JENNIFER: Uh-huh.

NIKKI: They have a workshop but they are not having a workshop
all the time for college stuff and they don't ever announce any-
thing about college. (November, 1993)

One year later:

JENNIFER: What do you think will stay with you about your experi-
ences in high school?

NIKKI: Everything.

JENNIFER: What's everything?

NIKKI: That one for instance. [She refers to Colleen. A young
woman I had tutored for a year, a friend of Nikki's.] . . . teach-
ers . . .everything. Friends, enemies.

JENNIFER: Teachers, so what about the teachers?

NIKKI: The good ones, the bad ones.

JENNIFER: Well, who are the good ones? I mean, don't give me
names, but what is a good teacher?

NIKKI: Someone who wants to help you learn. They push you.

JENNIFER: How do they do that?

NIKKI: Getting on your nerves every single day.

JENNIFER: Do they?

NIKKI: Yeah. Talk to you and stuff like that.

JENNIFER: Hmm . . . and what about the bad ones?

NIKKI: They just don't care. They just pass you for the hell of it.
(October 1994)

She equates teaching and communication. Good teachers speak to you "every
single day." Bad teachers are not even there; "they pass you for the hell of it";
"they just don't care." The implicit charge is that they pass you without teach-
ing you.

In "There Was No Place Left to Go," Nikki speaks of the dead-end evident in our conversation. She writes what is verifiable, what she has seen: "My friend ran away. I thought of her when I wrote the poem." She wrote the piece at home, one year after she took a workshop with Hermine.

> There was no place left to go.
> She ran away from home.
> She went everywhere.
> She went to her boyfriend's house
> he told her to leave
> he couldn't keep her.
> She went to family members' houses.
> But there was no one home.
> She's walking up and down the street.
> She saw a person getting robbed
> she was scared and nervous.
> A man came to her, he was talking to her
> and trying to rub up against her.
> She ran away from him.
> There was no place to go.
> She heard voices.
> There was no place to go.
> She walked to the nearest park.
> She saw a bench she laid down
> and went to sleep
> and when she awakened
> she was home
> because there was no place left to go.

In the end, Nikki arrives where she started—at home, because there is no place left to go. Her words evoke poet-activist Audre Lorde: "For the embattled/there is no place that cannot be home/nor is." And they evoke her perception that teachers leave you as you are. In the text and in real time, she sees few places to go.

Students failed to move progressively through the grades for a host of complex reasons. They were disaffected, resistant, and often overwhelmed. I will never forget the despondency in Nikki's voice as she gazed at her record, moved her finger down a list of classes, and whispered, "I have to take this class over, I have to take this class over."

JENNIFER: What can I do now to help you with English? [An NYU tutor has just placed her record in front of us. We can see every course she has ever taken, passed, and failed.]

NIKKI: I don't know. [Her voice is barely audible.] I got to take one, two, three, four. I got to take all of these classes over.

JENNIFER: What's this, English?

NIKKI: I'm taking this over already. I got to take math. I'm taking PE over.

JENNIFER: When are you going to do all of this?

NIKKI: Next semester. [Her voice becomes lower, she seems sad.] (October 1994)

For years I have thought about the reasons for Nikki's exhaustion and her failures. She temporarily disappeared within the school system. She was not alone. Sara, a veteran English teacher, once listed the reasons why her students arrived late: "They take their younger brothers and sisters to school or to do things around the house. Sometimes they have ambivalence about being in school. Sometimes they don't feel well or they got to sleep late the night before."

In the same conversation, I asked Sara if her students had common interests, and she nodded:

This semester, I started them on the topic of love and we read *Raisin in the Sun* for family love and now we're doing a study on Martin Luther King, Jr. for transcendental love and the love of God. There's a lot of juice in family love and, you know the ambiguities, pseudo love, if it's abusive. Is it really love even though it parades as love? I know that if I talk about these issues, I'm going to get them.

She went on to say that they often become excited, too excited, and talk at once. "I can't pay attention to them all." Then she shifted, abruptly, and told me about "the push-out rate," another reason why a steady progression through the grades breaks down.

SARA: Even though the registers are thirty to thirty-five, the class usually shakes out twenty to twenty-five, which is very interesting because that's where the push-out rate occurs.

JENNIFER: Push-out rate?

SARA: Well they [students] understand that the max that can learn is about twenty-three, even though the authorities don't understand that. So the weaker ones who are less able to get attention, they drop out. They may cut a particular class or they may cut out of school entirely. But they will know that there is not enough attention for them to learn and different ones usually drop out of different courses. In the classes they're stronger in they may struggle to stay in. But if they're not getting the attention they need and they think they are going to fail anyway and they feel jerky and they don't think they are going to get help, they just won't go. So the class tends to . . . I've seen this happen again and again and again over the years and I really believe it's like a group wisdom that happens. So that's why the program has extended itself. Most students take longer than four years.

JENNIFER: Most students in this school?

SARA: They don't get enough attention.

JENNIFER: In the class?

SARA: In the class. It's too large. (December 7, 1993)

Sara spends her own money for class resources, and she writes grants in order to secure additional funds for her courses. She scavenges library sales and street vendors for books. She contacts publishers for novels and volumes of poetry; then she carries these texts into the classroom on her back. Yet she describes and seems to accept a Darwinian process in which "the weaker ones drop out." Her attempts to focus on individuals are undermined by overcrowding, a lack of resources, classrooms without heat, and the acceptance of, or resignation to, a "push-out rate." After they are deemed harmless, students "who are less able to get attention, students who struggle to stay in" simply disappear.

Finding those who disappear is indeed a Herculean task. Rosters are in flux all year. Children emigrate from the Dominican Republic, Jamaica, Trinidad, Haiti, Malaysia, Panama, and West Africa. They arrive at the school's front door weeks after entering the country. The New York City Board of Education refers to them as "over-the-counter kids." Teachers like Sara struggle to give every child a book, despite the stream of students who move through their classes and the abject absence of resources. Others give up and watch the clock. Essayist and educator Richard Rodriguez describes the effect of academic neglect in "ghetto schools" in terms of an absence, the general lack of any effect at all.

> Radical educationalists . . . complain that ghetto schools "oppress" stu-
> dents by trying to mold them, stifling native characteristics. The truer cri-
> tique would be just the reverse: not that schools change ghetto students
> too much, but that while they might promote the occasional scholarship
> student, they change most students barely at all. (Rodriguez, 1983, p. 68)

His charge is amplified in the following exchange. Nikki's voice, its audible
whisper, extends Rodriquez's critique and ultimately indicates that the failure
to change students—in essence, the failure to teach them—is itself oppressive.

NIKKI: Some teachers don't explain nothing to you.
JENNIFER: What do they do?
NIKKI: They leave you as you are..

THE ARCHITECTURE OF SCHOOLING

UHS is housed in a beautiful building. Limestone decorates its light brick
façade, and near the entrance a stone frieze depicts an open book. These
marking clearly distinguish the site as a civic building, a school. During the
first half of the 20th century, government agencies reinforced the school's
civic role by decorating public space. In 1938, for example, the Works
Progress Administration donated a mural for the cafeteria. The following
year, it provided sculpted panels for the school's auditorium. In the mural,
Uncle Sam sits with a watering can on top of a donkey. The two symbols
(party and nation) are surrounded by circus animals and acrobats in various
stages of movement: climbing, running, flipping backwards. The characters
appear to move within the scene. According to Hugh Tyler, the head of the
WPA's mural division, "a sense of humor pervades the painting." The sculpt-
ed panels are more traditionally academic; female figures depict song, drama,
and literature. Both pieces were placed in rooms where all students gathered,
transforming them into places that belonged to citizens of the city—to the
families of Italian and Jewish girls who attended Commercial High School
and to the students themselves.

UHS's original design, and its symbolic significance, is covered by metal
grates and chicken wire. Fortification now marks entire neighborhoods; door
locks, barbed wire, and metal bars "epitomize the ghetto in America today,
just as back alleys, crowded tenements, and lack of playgrounds defined the
slum of the late nineteenth century" (Vergara, 1994, p. 102). Metal shutters
characterize the façades of banks and libraries, while bullet-proof Plexiglas

defines their interior (Vergara, 1997). Because the fear of crime has over-shadowed the fear of entrapment in poor and working-class city neighbor-hoods, I would like to extend Vergara's notion of ghetto symbolism and argue that bars have replaced 19th-century fire escapes as defining symbols of secu-rity. In private homes, metal windows block the fire escapes that still deco-rate the buildings that were once 19th-century tenements. Complete physi-cal containment conveys two messages: "This is a bunker and we are sealed off" and "Don't worry, the world won't come in and kill you" (Marshall Berman as cited in Vergara, 1997, p. 116). Bunkering is often deadly. In the early 1990s, a fire took the lives of two young girls in the Crown Heights neighborhood. Their bodies were found near a barred window next to an open toolbox. The two died searching for a way to open the gate that blocked their escape.

The fortification of city schools particularizes Vergara's historical com-parison, revealing how population control has changed over the past 60 years. In 1908, the overcrowding in Manhattan's Lower East Side was so great that schools seating 2,000 to 4,000 students were built on a yearly basis and still more were needed (Snyder, 1908). The annual increase in school enroll-ment heightened a concern for fire safety. C.B.J. Snyder,[3] one of New York City's principal architects of the time, subsequently claimed that Public School number 62, a model for architectural design, consisted of "four ele-vators and eight stairways . . . so arranged that the building may be vacated by its 4,000 occupants, using the stairway alone, in two minutes and forty seconds" (Snyder, 1908, p. 28). Snyder's concern with fire has become a prin-cipal's preoccupation with containing students due to potential violence. Thousands of students can no longer exit the building in minutes.

> JENNIFER: Do they let you go out? Go to the store, if you want to go to the store?
> NIKKI: No. They used to.
> JENNIFER: They used to?
> NIKKI: The thing is they never used to, but a lot of the security guards let people go out only if they'd bring them back some-thing to eat.
> JENNIFER: But there was a shooting right outside the library.
> NIKKI: There was? Inside the school?
> JENNIFER: No. Outside the school. In the neighborhood and after that shooting, [the principal] was even more concerned about students leaving the building. He made it harder for students to leave the building. (November 1993)

By 1993, the New York City Board of Education had spent more on an electromagnetic door and alarm system than on any other anti-violence program. The system was designed to keep all school doors locked from both inside and outside. School personnel opened all doors automatically with a special key but were instructed to do so only during a fire or other emergency (Dillon, 1993b). While I tutored at UHS, many of the school's five principle exits were locked to keep out trespassers.

Architecture not only reflects social fear; it reinforces collective fantasies. Glass has garnered the illusion of ascension, for example, or vast possibility. Numerous writers have relied on its visual effects to capture the hopes and disappointments of modernity (Buck-Morss, 1989). For Walter Benjamin, the glass-ceiling arcades of 19th-century Paris were symbols of modern duplicity, sustained by beliefs in infinite advancement. "The covered shopping arcades of the 19th century were Benjamin's central image because they were the precise material replica of the internal consciousness, or rather the unconscious of the dreaming collective" (Buck-Morss, 1989). The following images of schools reveal the extent to which the contents of an unconscious collective have changed.

From 1891 to 1923, Snyder built 200 H-shaped schools, each intended to bring light and air to children who spent much of their day in dark tenements (Roane, 1999, pp. B1, B8). Five years after he boasted that 4,000 students could exit one of his buildings in just under 3 minutes, he designed Bushwick High School, fashioning the ceiling of its lobby from iron and glass. Educational theorist John Devine states:

> One can only speculate on the extent to which the dreams and hopes of those earlier generations of mostly working-class youth of European extraction—whom one can imagine sitting in that auditorium in the early part of the century, gazing up at the sky—were fulfilled by the jobs they later occupied, mostly in New York City's factories. (Devine, 1996, p. 16)

Devine implies, and rightfully so, that school architecture fed dreams that were often denied. But they were sustained for a time by the physical layout of a building, namely an open lobby and ceilings that extended upward. We can imagine walking up the steps of a school, moving through an entrance. Once we are inside the building, a light that penetrates the glass forces our eyes up, past solid walls, to the sky, to air itself.

Glass and fire escapes enabled both an imagined and a literal exit: ways to see out or get out. They have been replaced by barbed wire, metal shutters, and sealed doors. Decades after the school's ceiling has been covered by plaster and green paint, Tanzania acknowledges that neighborhood high schools no longer symbolize hope: "Before they [students] get into the school, they automatically think: Oh my God, don't go to this school. I must be worth nothing." Do the children of Black immigrants harbor no illusions? If they do not, false hope [our metaphorical glass ceiling] has become a refusal to "dream," and solid foundations, automated factories, and traditional school buildings have entered a permanent state of disintegration. In the lobby where light once forced the eyes upward, students are scanned for weapons.

The perception of physical and psychological entrapment evident in Nessa's poetry may not have emerged in school, but her words reflect enclosure—the architecture of schooling must have solidified "The Thing Around":

> I'm scared of the thing around
> They're going to get me.
> I'm scared of what people say
> about me. They don't like me.
> Why? because I'm different
> from them. I come from a poor
> family. Clothes I have to wear
> everyday holes in my sneakers.
> I'm scared of what's going to
> happen to me.
> —Nessa, age 16

In her work, Nessa writes of an all-consuming object that will eventually "get her." The word "I" is repeated. It is nearly encircled in the first line: "I'm scared of the thing around." Nessa becomes the object of others, of their pronouncements, of their actions. Poverty defines her. In doing so, it seems to construct a fearful passivity. "I'm scared of what people [peers, classmates] say about me. They don't like me. Why? . . . because I come from a poor family." With the fifth line, the sentence structure changes. The "why" indicates that Nessa expects a response. She is conscious of an audience; she approximates dialogue, posing a question and providing the rationale. Through this structure, she places herself within a social context, and actively interprets everyday experience. The last line returns to a previous sentence structure: Nessa is the recipient of possible action—forever constrained by place and consciousness.

I once stood with a young man in the school cafeteria and stared at a mural that depicted former students. I don't remember what caught my eye initially, why I stood staring at the wall, but I remember the story that boy told. "Do you see him? Name's Hakeem. He was one of the toughest kids in this school. He was shot in the face. That eye's gone. Last I heard he was in jail. You see him? That's his girlfriend over there. The guy who painted this, he painted the popular kids." Former students stand looking back at the viewer, rigidly erect; "entombed in the paint and plaster of the walls," said a friend. There is no movement in these scenes, only the rough edges of a stance—arms straight to the side, legs stiff. The painter has portrayed teens who do nothing but wait.

"The Thing Around" has always seemed to mirror their entombment. Paradoxically, it effectively denies the creative, interactive self that articulates it.

THE THING AROUND/THE THING WITHIN: IMAGES OF ARMOR AND SANCTUARY

Following the practice of her teacher, Ruth Danon, Hermine asked students to write in class. She noted, "Danon believes that when you create and exercise for an entire class, you are creating an experience to which all respond. The structure of a group contained a situation. Exercises, when put together, allow you to go beyond the constraints of usual ways of thinking." Like Danon, she introduced exercises that forged a collective experience and structured or contained the group. The group itself provided a sanctuary outside of the school's architecture and its criminal binary. The poetry became another space within the school, but, unlike the structure of a contained group, it had the potential either to constrain a writer or to liberate her. Hermine asked teens to live in the world, to capture it in concrete detail, and she elicited poems that did not correspond to anything "in reality." Her exercises pushed them beyond commonsensical constraints, but they could also lead them to internal traps, including fear, sadness, and rage. By giving them permission to mix natural and supernatural phenomena, she incited them to change how the world appeared, and through these perceptions they could enter places beyond fortification. Through writing, students had *the choice* to exit entrapment. Poetry was a late-20th-century escape route.

In "The Troll Is Loose," inspired by an assignment to imagine a physical metamorphosis, the character of the writer/subject is active. Transformation invokes a creative freedom that allows Nessa to rename herself and the world around her. However, the ultimate image she constructs is one of immobilization. The author has devised a poetic sanctuary, but remains frozen within it.

THE TROLL IS LOOSE

I was jumping rope and something weird happened.
I was jumping real fast and it happened. I turned into a troll.
I had big ugly eyes a big flat nose,
my hair was sticken up. My skin was all bumpy.
I was the worst creature alive.
Everybody was just standing there in total shock of what happened.
And I don't know what happened to me. I started chasing them.
Everybody was yelling help help the troll is loose.
I started making a face and then I turned into a moving tree.
I started knocking people over. And yelling please make it stop
please. And then I turned into a sculpture
and everybody else went back to a normal life.

Nessa is violent, "the worst creature alive." She doesn't want this new form, nor does she get to keep it: "I started knocking people over. And yelling please make it stop. And then I turned into a sculpture." With each transformation, the writer becomes increasingly stationary until, finally, she is a sculpture—cold, hard and immobile.

Throughout the text, Nessa is subject to her own body, subject to its violence and then to its petrification. Each physical manifestation becomes a prison, what the writer refers to as "the thing around"—not poverty, not the police, not UHS's security force and not those who jump her. External threats have permeated her consciousness, her physical existence. In a discussion of women's poetry, Alicia Ostriker states: "Women do not really want to be secure, hard dispassionate objects. They hate it. The flat inflections of their voices say they hate it" (Ostriker, 1986, p. 87).

If Nessa despises petrification, others accept its normality. Perhaps teens expect images of fortification in a school where people "just jump at you for nothing." Yet Nessa moves away from an aggressive persona. She is protected, but immobile. Her exterior can only be defensive. The price of such armor may be self-entrapment: "a prison sanctuary which prevents us from entering another's mind to know what it is like for her there" (Ostriker, 1986, p. 171).

Jhoy wrote "Untitled" after Hermine asked her to see herself in a particular place. "Close your eyes," she said to the class. "Notice what is around you and now go to some other place, real or imagined." In the poem, Jhoy mentions sorrow and describes the darkening sun in order to convey a mood.

UNTITLED

1.
The trees are slow in moving to the wind.
The sun is gently shining down, bathing the hills in light.
I am happy.

2.
A cloud drifts across the sun darkening the sun,
Darkening the land.
The cloud passes on but the land is still dark,
Or is it darker?

3.
The trees are tired men coming home from battle,
Or battles?
The land is burnt black.
There is no wind.
Now there is no sunshine,
And I am sad.

Jhoy entraps herself within the mood and moves beyond it. The skill, this kind of control over language and imagery, is invaluable, for it forces the writer to rely on her imaginary power—her ability to conjure a world and then escape it. When I asked Hermine why she devised this exercise, she told me, "I was trying to get at their ability to find worlds within themselves." Finding the world within, that internal landscape, gives young people a chance to transcend the physical and temporal reality of everyday life.

Initially, I read "My Abstract Life" as evidence of the dehumanizing poses apparent at the school. But after years of listening, I began to hear the poem's flexibility. Tanzania does not merely record her experience of objectification, she resists that experience.

MY ABSTRACT LIFE

My sense is your chaos
My chaos makes sense.
I am destined to be
Lost.
No one knows my world
Drag me to the asylum

so I can be amongst
my brilliant peers
They are, you know,
brilliant people.
Am I chaotic in
a world that's supposed
to make sense?
Am I sensible in a
chaotic world?
A diamond in the ruff?
Am I . . . ?
What am I here for?
To be laughed at?
Ridiculed?
Scorned?
Labeled?
Judged?
What?
What is my place
in this semi-chaotic
and semi-sensible
world?
To be pointed at
and talked about?
You look at me
because you want to know.
If I speak, I am to be
quieted.
If I move, I am to be
stopped.
No one knows my name,
no one knows anything about
me.
Yet they can tell stories
about me.
I don't question their
actions any more, I let
it be. I have succumbed
to the madness.
I have become madness.

"What is my place" in an institution where "no one knows my name" in a world where "you look at me because you want to know." In Tanzania's abstract (reduced) life, others judge and label her, but do not know her. They look and tell stories, but comprehend nothing. Abstraction dehumanizes; yet madness becomes a comfort relative to the assault of being superficially named.

Tanzie positions *chaos/sense*, and *I/world* in close proximity. Her inverted questions (lines 12–16) point to a permeable boundary between these states. Simple declarative statements would have set up dichotomies; questions introduce a slipperiness between sense and chaos, *I* and *world*. Madness completely dissolves the concept of an internal-external divide. It obliterates consciousness, providing "the freedom of the wholly mad/to smear & play with her madness" (Ostriker, 1986, p. 144). Tanzania chooses such "freedom" rather than consenting to remaining encaged. Madness makes her blissfully unaware of the chaotic world in which she is judged, labeled, and scorned. The boundary that she places between herself and her environment is no longer invaded because it is no longer recognized; and within an all-encompassing state, "I have become madness," the embodiment of the self cannot be profaned through having to submit to debasing stances (Goffman, 1961, p. 23).

The act of writing, like madness, reconfigures the boundary between self and world. But while the mad stay within their own irrational visions, the poet moves between experiencing the external constraints of a physical world and composing that experience. By writing, Tanzania objectifies her own entrapment, articulates its conditions, and thereby creates a weapon with which to fight institutional violence. Within "My Abstract Life," there are thus two subject positions: the author is subject to language (labels, judgments) and she undercuts that subjection by recording her objectification. The poem is a place "where language has [us] at its disposition" (Ricoeur, 1974, p. 93). Yet it confers control.

Strong poems are empathetically dual (Ostriker, 1986). "Drag me to the asylum" means what it says, but it also means the opposite. I have read "asylum" as a site where individuals are constrained and forced to act in ways that are incompatible with previous perceptions of the self. I have come to read it as a search for sanctuary. Underneath the author's sense of entrapment is a tone that screams refusal. While here the refusal suggests a desire to imagine what cannot be imagined in the poem itself, student writers do come to name and transcend oppression.

NOTES

1. As a professor of education at Brooklyn College, I returned to UHS to observe student teachers. One of the student teachers spontaneously retold this story, after I asked, "How was your day?"

2. I have taken this title from a book by Raymond Callahan.

3. Snyder was superintendent of New City School Buildings from 1891 to 1923—a time of heavy immigration.

CHAPTER 4

Escape Routes

> You've left me with the hate
> I never asked for
> Rapist. Racist. They look almost the same.
> Rapist. Racist. They are the same.
> —Tanzania

In schools, like UHS, the language of security and sanctity accompanies the use of high-tech police tactics. Giuliani reminds us that "school is a sacred place," then promises to install walk-through metal detectors in New York's most violent schools (Sexton, 1994, p. A27). To achieve sanctity, the city posts red-lettered warning signs. Everyone walking up the stone steps of UHS reads:

> All persons entering this building are required to submit to a metal detector scan and a personal search, if necessary, to ensure that weapons are not brought into this building. Bags and parcels also may be searched by means of metal detector devices, by hand, or otherwise.

The sign, visible daily, dims the significance of the UHS pledge, administered to every graduating class:

> With gratitude to the school, I pledge: As a graduate student of UHS, to cherish thoughts of the UHS "Experience"; as a citizen to work both alone and with others to try to improve my city and its surroundings; and as an American to obey my country's laws, according to my conscience, and to try to make its constitution work for each and every citizen.

"To work both alone and with others . . . to obey my country's laws *according to my conscience*": the phrases connect responsibility to the formation a democratic self-government. Civic instruction, specifically discussions that link autonomy, consciousness, and democracy, has been diluted by simple commands: "[A]ll persons . . . are required to submit to a metal detector scan." This dilution reflects the amalgamation of routines and architectural designs outlined in Chapter 3.

Locked doors and electronic surveillance—physical structures—made potential criminality appear like a given. They helped constitute the beliefs and practices in which students, teachers, guards, and administrators thought and acted. They were, in other words, ideological. Assuming a criminal stance consumed individual student bodies—dictating the position of one's legs, hands, fingers—but it deemphasized movement for the sake of efficiency. Holding one's book, listening to the binder crack, and turning a page leads to a sense of self that must be incompatible with the effect of waiting while others watch that book through an x-ray machine as it becomes a photographic negative, an object without dimension, a flattened portrait of your possessions. According to Louis Althusser, physical submissions construct particular subjectivities. He cites the following prescription as a demonstration of this: "Kneel down, move your lips and you will believe" (Pascal, cited in Althusser, 1971, p. 168). Walk past a uniformed guard and you will remember that violence is possible. If we accept Althusser's claim that ideology has a material existence, that it inheres in bodily routines, we see a shift from efforts to construct obedient subjects to the acceptance and continuous depiction of criminal suspects. One teen saw the effects of scanning as follows.

> These metal detectors . . . they are another way of teaching us how stupid we are. They are another way of teaching us how low and poor and degraded we are. I don't look like no criminal. Just because I carry myself with a certain amount of confidence, I am scanned day in and day out. I don't knock them for what they're doing, but don't do it to me . . . when you teach a cat he's a dog, he's gonna act like a dog. If you stop teaching cats they're dogs, they're gonna act like cats. (Educational Video Center, 1993)

For girls, police tactics lead to multiple kinds of labeling. Walk-through metal detectors, x-ray machines, and handheld scanners immediately define young women as harmless or dangerous. In doing so, they exemplify an institutional authority that functions according to one set of policing standards. Guards complicate UHS's security practices by acting according to gender roles that stem from personal desire and cultural norms. According to Nessa,

"Security guards go behind the stairs with the children, with the students. Talking to them, touching them."

After they are sorted according to sexual and criminal norms, young women struggle to hold onto their integrity, and to a sense of self that emerges at home. Tanzania once told me, "We were reared as girls. We were told to keep our legs closed." They were also told to cover their bodies, and to "behave" in public. "When you are out of your house, you got to know how to control yourself because you're going to be in the public and especially for girls—pretty girls should be seen and not heard" (Michelle, a 16-year-old from Guyana).

Standing with arms stretched and legs apart often leads to a disassociation of the self. In a 1999 interview with me, Tanzania said: "I was asked to see the scanning as normal, nothing more. By bringing the girl who said 'let it be nothing' into existence, I pushed the self that was hurt away." In the following dialogue, she uses metaphors that depict degradation, and renders a detailed image of her body as it assumes a criminal stance. The images embedded in her language, and the stance itself, set the parameters for a negotiation of self-perception.

JENNIFER: Were you ever scanned?

TANZANIA: Yeah. I hated it.

JENNIFER: Why did you hate it?

TANZANIA: First of all the guards think that because they have a uniform on they are above all others in the school. [Seconds of silence] I hate it because I have to put myself down I have to put my hands out [she places her hand on the table in front of us, fingers are stretched apart]. I hate it I don't feel right. I feel out of my element."

JENNIFER: What do you have to do?

TANZANIA: I have to stand straight, legs apart, I have to take everything out of my pockets.

JENNIFER: Do girls take off their jewelry?

TANZANIA: If it's not visible. [She paused for a moment, then continued.] Stand straight for a few minutes, having my hands in front of me and out stretched my legs apart, it's very uncomfortable, I felt embarrassed amongst everybody else. I don't like that feeling. It's not good. It's not a productive way to start off school. (January, 1994)

"I have to put myself down"—those words point to feelings of degradation that are inconsistent with previous conceptions of Tanzania's self. In fact, the phrase "I feel out of my element" implies a temporary rift in the environment she normally inhabits.

Six months later, Tanzania illustrates what it means to be "out of my element." This time, she couples scanning with the image of a shield and sexual intimacy.

> JENNIFER: You said that when you're scanned you feel out of your
> element. What does that mean? What element?
> TANZANIA: I feel like they are trying to get to know my body.
> JENNIFER: Through scanning?
> TANZANIA: Yeah. Not only that. You know what I think it is, I
> hear the comments or I see the looks from the guards to
> other girls. And through that and through the scanning,
> they get closer than they can ever get in a normal way
> because they can look at a girl from a distance and lust after
> her. In a way, they are trying to take my shield away because
> with the scanning they are looking for something I might
> have concealed. It's a secretive thing. I feel like they're trying
> to know my secrets. They want to find out secrets that many
> students don't have. They're [students] not concealing any-
> thing.

The phrase "they get closer than they can ever get in a normal way" is additional evidence of a forced interpersonal contact. But in this case, the searcher as well as the search penetrates the boundary, "the shield," that Tanzania has placed between her body and her surroundings. "They are looking for something I might have concealed" implies that she believes they are looking for much more than metal; they are searching for anything extraordinary or excessive, not in her bag, but on her body and in her imagination: "They're trying to know my secrets." When I asked her how this made her feel, she replied, "naked." In UHS, seeing (through a criminal search) indicates more than visual recognition. It yields power and vulnerability. It is, as a friend suggested, "like seeing the bones of my son's x-ray"—the bits and pieces of oneself that you cannot control rendered visible.

In a school where the criminal and the sexualized female subject are continually represented, a shield enables young women to regain some control over presentation of the self. In the conversation I cite below, scanning restricts Tanzania's autonomy, even as it elicits her defiance; shielding ultimately emerges from routine physical submission.

JENNIFER: Remember you compared scanning to a man staring at you. Are the two similar because you do not know how you are being looked at?

TANZANIA: There's a difference. Before I saw him staring at me, I felt so free. I looked up and that ruined my happiness. I couldn't think. I couldn't even type. I was free. When I saw him staring at me, I was instantly caged in. With the scanning, I knew what would happen. I knew how to be. I knew not to be free [moments of silence]. And now you'll ask me, "What do I mean by free?" Free in my thoughts and in my behavior. It wasn't like I'd be caught off guard. If I was scanned or not— not everyone was scanned everyday—I was ready to stare at them. Actually it was more of an attitude than actually staring. I felt important. Scanning wouldn't let me feel less important.

Unlike the sporadic gaze that "instantly cages," scanning engenders an attitude. "I knew what would happen. I knew how to be. I knew not to be free." This absence of freedom does not reflect a physical relationship of constraint, but an internalized state. Tanzania is ready to be scanned; she is never caught off guard; she stares back. Preparedness protects her integrity and it ensures confinement. She raises a shield with the realization that she is not free; she raises it within a cage.

Through multiple forms of expression, teens hid from others, asserted violent personas, and explored individual identities. Poetry, however, allowed them a measure of transcendence, a means of moving beyond the cage— beyond the constraints of time, place, and ordinary consciousness.

DON'T HURT ME ANYMORE

As I read Tanzania's poem "Don't Hurt Me Anymore," I was reminded of her narration of the bodily stance that young Black women assume as they enter the doors of UHS: "Stand straight, hands in front of me, legs apart." Rape, the controlling metaphor in her work, uncovers the twin abuses—sexual and racial—that the writer encounters in school.

DON'T HURT ME ANYMORE

Don't follow me
like a rapist stalks his prey

Don't quiet the words I have to say
like a rapist covers the mouth of his victim to hold back what
    she must say
Don't rip savagely apart my dreams
as a rapist rips the clothes off his victim
Don't throw me down when I try to get up
like a rapist throws down his victim
when she tries to escape
Don't hit me and beat me
when I struggle to learn and survive
like a rapist beats his victim
when she struggles to break free
Don't threaten me to keep my mouth quiet
Don't pin my thoughts down
like a rapist pins the arms of his victim
on the cold concrete
Don't heave your hateful thoughts down on me
like a rapist heaves his body down on his victim
Don't thrust anymore of your sick ideas into my head
like a rapist thrusts his body
into his screaming victim
Don't force me to say what you want
like a rapist forces his victim
to perform debasing sexual acts
Don't leave me crying without a shred of confidence to go on
like a rapist leaves his victim feeling cold,
in a dark secluded place
without a shred of dignity to continue living
Don't make me second guess myself
when I know I have the right to speak
like the rape victim second guesses
if she deserves what happened to her
You've left me with the hate
I never asked for
Rapist. Racist. They look almost the same.
Rapist. Racist. They are the same.

Rape, as a metaphor, allows Tanzie to speak of psychological oppression. First
indirectly: "Don't pin my thoughts down like the rapist pins the arms of his
victim." Then directly: "Rapist. Racist. They are the same." Paradoxically, in

a conversation about the effects of scanning, Tanzie retracts her insights and inverts her critique against herself. Stripped of metaphor, she denies that the stance objectifies her.

> JENNIFER: What were you thinking of when you said: "I feel like they're trying to get to know my body"?
> TANZANIA: You know, I feel like I'm hearing the words of a paranoid person. I listen and say am I really paranoid about sex? A lot of people tell me that's a phobia for me. (April, 1995)

She turns on herself; she is simply "paranoid." The self-assurance evident in poetry disappears. While the black and white of a story line inside conversation leaves little room to hide, poetry opens a space for social commentary and self-acceptance. The poetic "I" is always a persona. It enables a writer to turn around and say "that's not me" without repudiating her feelings, her knowledge, her experience. Student poets use this understanding to reveal multiple dimensions of themselves and to subvert institutional practices of criminal surveillance that otherwise reduce them to a single, dehumanizing identity.

Three years after she heard the words of "a paranoid person," Tanzania offered a complex explanation for why she collapsed "rapist" and "racist" in "Don't Hurt Me Anymore." By this time, she had spent 2 years in college. Her analysis reflected the associational thought process evident in her original work, and years of academic training.

> Racism and rape are constraints that can affect me at anytime;
> both are sporadic, wild, yet planned and pointed. If you eliminate
> specifics, they are the same. One would be left feeling the same:
> confused, hurt (somehow I'm at fault, somehow this is deserved).
> The mouth replaces the penis. (January, 1998)

Rape, the controlling metaphor in Tanzania's poem, allows her to uncover twin images of oppression, years before she articulates the connection in prose. Through poetry, she reads the world with great sophistication and sensitivity—temporarily unimpeded by the constraints of her own consciousness and social perceptions.

Tanzania was not the only student whose work expressed unconventional wisdom—who wrote with a knowledge and sophistication never articulated in conversation or prose. I have come to believe that poetry unleashed perceptions of which the writer was not completely aware in ordinary consciousness. In the poem below, Shakeya conveys an insight rarely, if ever, acknowledged in school or home. Hermine had read Russell Edson's "Oh My God I'll Never Get Home," a poem about a man whose body parts fall off in the road. Then she told the class, "be as silly as you can possibly be," and Shakeya wrote "I Went Into Her Brain."

> I pulled out her cerebrum
> Fed it to her child.
> I pulled out her cerebellum
> Fed it to her 2nd child.
> I pulled out her medulla
> Fed it to her 3rd child.
> Then
> I went in her neck.
> I pulled out her esophagus
> Fed it to her 1st child.
> She sucked the juicy blood
> off of it.
> I went in the chest.
> Pulled out both lungs
> Chopped them up into
> Pieces fed it to the
> 2nd and 3rd child.
> Used the blood as juice.
> She said she
> would do anything for her kids.

Earlier that semester Shakeya had been asked to write about a hero, and had written an essay about her mother, the person she most admired, the woman who raised kids alone, the woman she would like to become. She wrote that essay within the framework of a linear format and through a conscious effort to make order; she worked slowly through a progression, constantly aware of the mother she wanted to present, and trying to write respectfully. She wrote her poem through a playful experimentation with language. Ultimately, "I Went Into Her Brain" reveals a dark reality, an understanding that children devour their mother's body. The poem, in this instance, is "language surprised in the act of changing into meaning"—because, in this instance, language is largely unconscious, it draws from the unconscious and is, therefore, not in the form of explication (Kunitz, 1993, pp. 1–2). When I told Hermine about Shakeya's essay, she said that the push toward linearity does not always allow complex associations. I have concluded that this push does not easily allow us to go beyond conscious intention. Connection to the deeper workings of consciousness enabled Shakeya to discover and write about the selfless mother/hero who is pulled, chopped, and fed to her kids.

WHEN I WALK DOWN THE HALL:
PROFILING AND OTHER PERFORMANCES

High school students acted within extant architectural (and ideological) structures. They disguised themselves through dress and graffiti. After conducting interviews in an urban high school, the assistant director of a dropout prevention program wrote:

> As we [researcher and guard] were talking, a student passed through the station without slowing down, throwing his arms up in an act of surrender. . . . He might as well have said "fuck you" to everyone, but he just laughed and said: "Go ahead. Stop me. I'm clean." I looked at the guard: "Sitting here with you it's amazing how many students don't bring anything to school? Do you think this is a conscious effort to beat the system (avoid x-ray screening)?" Laughing, he responded: "Definitely! It's hilarious. I mean sometimes they bring some food but not books. I would guess about 20% bring absolutely nothing to school" (Lucas, 1995, p. 203).

For 20% of a student body, behavior seems to be determined, or at least shaped, by electronic surveillance and not academic pressure. Erasing and asserting the self through disguise, or persona, can be interpreted as oppositional, a metaphorical "fuck you" to the guards and the institution at large. It can also be interpreted as a means of protection in a school where students "jumped each other just to get a rep." The piece below followed a series of creative exercises. Hermine asked her tenth graders to tell a story that happened at home. To complete the assignment, they were told to rely on sensory memory, to note what they saw and heard. A week later, I modified the idea by telling Nessa that I wanted to see the streets that surround UHS through her eyes.

When I was going
home on Friday
a whole bunch of
boys jump this one boy for his
bookbag. They punch his eye

which gave him
a black eye. And
then they kicked him
and punched him
in the stomach.

The possibility of physical violence influenced individual expression. Wearing an oversized hood was never simply a reaction to UHS policy: students wore hoods to forge a tough pose. After reading my fieldnotes, Tanzania detailed how students use ski masks, caps, and oversized hoods to construct a public presence; these articles of clothing, which students refer to as "props," play a role in performance.

> TANZANIA: Why do they [students] hide their faces?
> JENNIFER: It was a cold day. Kids had their sleeves down. I don't
>   think all of them had gloves. They were stamping their feet
>   and waiting for that bell . . . But I've seen kids wear jackets
>   over their heads on days that are not cold.
> TANZIE: It's a cool thing. At one point it was a cool thing. "Oh
>   wow I don't want to be recognized by the cops, so let me do
>   this." Believe me I've seen it before. I've seen it a lot. I've seen
>   it on my block.
> JENNIFER: They do it so they're not recognized? But the school
>   knows who they are.
> TANZIE: No, no. It's not for the school. It's for the other kids. Like
>   oh what's he hiding from? He must be bad. O.K. he's cool. I
>   like him. He deserves respect. He's hiding from something.

Her explanation complicated my perception of clothing as a means to hide from "the school." She sees teens who want to be seen not by adults but by "the other kids." She sees the mask of an outlaw: "What's he hiding from? He must be bad. O.K. he's cool. I like him. He deserves respect." Self-erasure exists alongside a desire to be known as "bad." Clothing may have been a shield that served as a boundary between self and world, but it was also a way to strike a pose. Tanzie described the pose, in more detail, in a conversation about violence.

> TANZANIA: Remember I said you could see if a person is going to
>   be loud or not. You can see from their behavior. I knew they
>   [boys on a city bus] were going to start something.

JENNIFER: How did you know?

TANZANIA: Just by their appearance [she draws out the last word].

JENNIFER: How did they appear? Describe it.

TANZANIA: O.K. the cool look, call it, is umm is Guess, Tommy
Hilfiger, lots of gold, not a lot but enough gold. You wear your
clothes a certain way. And there's a walk, a cool walk.

JENNIFER: What does it look like?

TANZANIA: It looks like a damn limp that's what it looks like. Looks
like you got shot in the hip. And they think it's cool. It looks
ridiculous and you know you don't walk like that. (May 1995)

In his discussion of style politics, Robin Kelley argues that dress is both a
reflection of the individual's desire to define his or her own identity and a
reflection of social processes: "Young men wear starter jackets, hoodies, L. A.
Raiders caps, baggy khaki pants, and occasionally gold chains not only
because they are in style, but because it enables them to create their own
identity—one that defines them as rebels" (1994, p. 205). Kelley then sug-
gests that an "implicit acceptance of an outlaw status" emerged from capital-
ist transformation and the militarization of Black Los Angeles. As in L. A.,
aggressive policing and unemployment existed alongside tough poses. Young
people won respect from each other when they sported a "cool look" and hid,
or at least pretended to hide, from the cops.

Social relations (those defined by weapon searches, police logs, and
access machines) and a teenage desire to assert identity were always evident
in the hallway, a nomadic place that was often crowded between periods.
Police questioned students in school as they walked to class. And while class-
es were in session, guards chased them during "sweeps," a term borrowed
from police lexicon and used to describe the removal of all students from
school corridors. These attempts were rarely a deterrent. Teens perceived the
hallway as a place to be seen; they wrote their names on walls and referred to
walking the corridor as "profiling"—the word was also used by the police,
part of the language of a surveillance that emerged from racial stereotyping.
The term, like the corridor itself, was contested: students want to be seen in
"name brand clothing," and they "profile" to define themselves. On the other
hand, guards "profile" and define them as dangerous, as trouble, and as a pos-
sible public nuisance. Perhaps more importantly, the term "sweep," like the
term "profiling," indicates the extent to which students and guards, rather
than students and teachers, battle for control of the corridor, a public space.

Nessa associates profiling and a tough pose with name-brand clothing—
Guess and Damage. In her poem, "When I Walk Down the Hallway," name-

brand clothes become forms of mystical protection: without them you are perceived as weak. Clothing thus produces a one-dimensional surface through which teens see themselves and others.

> When I walk down the hallway, I see people looking at all the people that's different. If you don't look suitable, people want to jump you because you don't wear Guess, Damage, etc. You have to wear name brand clothes. People just come to school to show off their stuff. If you look at somebody, they want to jump you. People think if you wear all these clothes that you can beat up people.
> —Nessa, age 16

The writer is not explicitly beaten. Nor does she sport a protective image; she simply sees. After the first line of the text, "I" is effaced. By writing through "you," she seems to maintain an omniscient perspective, to remain outside the divide she has established between those who commit violence and those who fall victim to it. Yet this omniscience is ultimately threatened by the repetition of "you." The second person is mentioned eight times, and in five instances "you" is a victim. The subject's repeated role in this position makes me believe that Nessa has masked herself, through the use of an indirect pronoun.

After writing "When I Walk Down the Hallway," Nessa wrote another prosaic piece in which she describes the connection between clothing and violence. I did not give her a direct prompt, but the work clearly attempts to record what she has seen. In the new piece, clothing is evocative, but it no longer acts as a shield.

> I was walking downtown by Conway and I saw people jump somebody because their clothes were bummy. They beat her up, took her money out of her pocket and ran away. It was 3:00 o'clock. There were 100 people around but nobody did anything to stop it. Why? Because they didn't care because it was mostly boys. I think the violence should stop.
> —Nessa

Again Nessa observes a scene. She is not beaten, but the structure of the piece reminds me of "The Thing Around," a poem that describes "everyday holes" and other people's derision. In both texts, young women are reduced to objects—dismissed or physically attacked because of their appearance. Syntax itself relegates them to an object position.

They don't like me.
Why? because I'm different

Nessa's prose poems reminded me of the countless young women I have seen at their desks wearing heavy coats, nearly invisible in the classroom. Like the women of these texts, they are surrounded not by hostile crowds but by dress. I remember talking to Vera, a silent teen, who was sitting in an English class, her body enwrapped in a large winter coat. It was spring and I asked if she was cold. "No. I just wear it." I could see her face, but little else. Unlike the girls in Nessa's work, she uses dress to erase part of herself.

JENNIFER: What do you do after school?
VERA: Stay in my room. My mother doesn't allow me to go out.
     She says the streets are too violent.
JENNIFER: What do you do at home?
VERA: Sometimes I look out the window. I see kids my age. I want
     to go out, but it's better that I don't.

The coat, like the room, protected and imprisoned her. Nadia, the young woman who wrote about the shooting incident in Chapter 1, often covered herself in a large coat too. When asked to imagine herself as an animal and to write from that experience, she transcended the confines of dress, her neighborhood, and her own body:

Horse, Summer breeze
I can feel the swiftness of the breeze,
that's why I was named summer breeze

     The laps of my curly hair flow like
a river down the spine of my neck
my body is warm with golden fur
spreaded across the hooves of my legs.
The day is wonderful and gay
The summer breeze is rushing through
the storms of the bay.
Slow down I cannot I must not,
with hooves carrying me far away.
dash I run through the forest of the unknown.
Jumping through the rivers of Shogone.
I feel free and fast

No one dear to cast me down.
I am beauty with four legs
I am swift through open flower pegs
I will run all the days of my life
I will taste the water and take a dive.
Summer breeze cannot be catched
for I am no longer the Prisoner of Men.

The choices she makes in language and syntax converge to move the poem and to give us a visceral experience of the horse running: "slow down I cannot I must not . . . Dash I run through the forest unknown." According to Hermine, Nadia was one of the most gifted writers at UHS. She wrote often, filling notebooks with stories that mimicked the gothic novels she read at home. In poetry workshops, she could draw on memory or write about her surroundings. She consistently played with language and syntax to affect mood, rhythm, and imagery. The sensuality and virtuosity of her language was consistently stunning. But more than any other poem, "Horse, Summer Breeze" counters confinement, a reality she experienced all too often; more than any other poem, this one expressed free movement.

Without figurative language, the use of persona, or metaphor, students remained within their immediate environment, profiling or cloaking themselves and sometimes disappearing within daily social interactions. In the following comments, Tanzania notes her own invisibility; she describes her response to a security guard who does not see her even as he touches her.

> You know the guard. He's very tall. Don't like him. One day he was pushing students. Students were just being pushed out of the cafeteria. He didn't realize he was pushing me until I started screaming, "Why are you touching me, why are you pushing me?" He said, "Oh, I'm sorry. I'm sorry. I want to get you out of the cafeteria." He thought I was going to be herded out of the cafeteria like every other student. I'm not cattle to be herded out. And I said, "You don't even realize what you're doing." [Voice becomes louder.] He didn't realize he was just pushing me out of the cafeteria. (Interview with Tanzania, January 1994)

Touch, normally an intimate and individualizing means of communication, does not individualize in this case. The guard does not feel Tanzania; he feels the body of a crowd, a crowd that he attempts to contain. For him, touch is a means of curtailing a potentially unruly population. It preserves "the herd," even as it works directly on individual bodies. Tanzania subsequently disappears and as part of a group that must be "herded out," she becomes "every other student."

Some students intentionally hid from school authorities—assuming their own complicity. I once accompanied a senior down to the library after he asked for help on a research project. As I stood beside him, he approached the librarian. He stammered, lowered his eyes, and spoke. "I'd like to take out this book." "So sign here for it." The boy then turned to me and in a whisper asked, "Do I give my real name?" (Fieldnotes, April 1993). In an environment in which all are suspect, hiding is a means of shielding oneself from blame and responsibility; the strategy is often employed automatically.

I repeatedly saw the following image over a 3-year period and have come to read it as an expression of extreme alienation and a desire for protection—a belief that if you hide from the world, the world cannot hurt you.

> As I pass through the cafeteria on my way to class, a lone boy sits slumped over one of the lunch tables. His shoulders are hunched, drawing his body inward. He wears a hooded jacket, several sizes too large, and a cap. He has pushed the brim of his cap down over his eyes. Only his mouth remains visible. (Fieldnotes, December 14, 1994)

The boy's use of clothing and his bodily pose erase any trace of individuality. We cannot see a face; hence there is no persona. Given the body's withdrawn position (shoulders hunched, upper body drawn inward), the hooded jacket indicates more than just the erasure of individual characteristics; it enables a physical disappearance—it is death-like.

His response stands in opposition to Tanzania's insistence that "I am not cattle." The young man dresses up as an object and effectively melts into a scene. This symbolic disappearance mimics reality. Students physically disappear: "literally exported from the school scene through safety transfers, suspensions, dropouts, injuries, jail, or in the extreme, death" (Devine, 1996, p. 115).

THE DISTANCE BETWEEN VIOLENCE AND LANGUAGE: LOGGING AND TAGGING A DANGEROUS PERSONA

Fear (predicated on real and perceived danger) overwhelms civic instruction and the promotion of civic duty, just as it overwhelms any social reproduction of labor. In the following conversation, school authorities convert a blunt metal scissors into a potential weapon, and render the student who carries it a suspect, effacing her individuality as someone who volunteered for an after-school arts project, and who craves the regularity of a brown pleated skirt.

JHOY: Oh. There was one time when I came to school and I put my bag through the metal detector and after months they finally found scissors that was in there. They were blunt, old metal scissors. They brought me to the dean's office. They had me logged, took my scissors away, and told me not to bring them to school again.

JENNIFER: The scissors?

JHOY: I heard they took scissors and box cutters away but I was putting this bag through a metal detector for months [accents last word of sentence]. He finally found it and he kept it and said you need a note from your art teacher saying you need this.

NESSA: Oh, my God.

JHOY: If I brought a scissors or anything that would cut, can be used for cutting, or can stab somebody—and it's for art. If it's for art you need a note from the teacher. Or they will take it from you and log you.

TANZANIA: Logging?

JHOY: They told me that since it's the first time I was logged, it's a warning. Otherwise they call your parents or something.

JENNIFER: When they log you they take your name down?

JHOY: Yeah. They asked me my name, my school ID number. They have the date.

Blunt, old metal scissors evoke scenes of childhood innocence: cutting, eye-hand coordination, our first awkward attempts to make anything. It is stripped of that meaning when "they take it away and log you," when it becomes a weapon that can cut or stab. "For art" recedes into the background; for art is a secondary defining feature. The blunt old metal scissors is a child's scissors while we are permitted to free associate, while it remains embedded in our memory.

The language of the log is a place where violence and reason (if it can cut somebody, they take it away) come together simultaneously. Ultimately authorities remake truth by relying on technology and ignoring subjective experience. By arresting the moment of the scissors discovery, security guards and the dean of discipline can transform its use and, more importantly, they can transform the girl who possesses it. As part of a system that profiles sup-posed deviance, Jhoy is reduced to the entry of a recording; she is rendered suspect. This type of reductive representation parallels the symbolic erasure of the student body through clothing. Students undoubtedly choose their dress, and do not choose to walk under a metal detector. But as the institu-tion simplifies them, they simplify themselves.

Graffiti asserts the power to disfigure. Like the outlaw's mask, it can be a symbol of a forbidden identity, a "token of a self-imposed exile" (Hebdige, 1988, p. 2). Norman Mailer explains the relationship between "writing" and social constraint as "[Y]our presence on their presence . . . hanging your alias on their scene" (Mailer cited in Hebdige, p. 3). The quotation clarifies the link between ideological processes (of schooling) and agency: UHS students write about what prevails. They trace violent personas on public corridors, tagging or writing names that often express some affiliation with a gang. I have seen aliases like "Trigger" and "Dangerous" written with thick markers on corridor walls, scratched into glass, penned on visitor stickers (the ones that begin with: "Hello my name is"), and attached to fluorescent lights. The irony is unmis-takable: The tag makes us (all readers) aware of what is and what ought to be. "Hello my name is 'Dangerous'" holds civility and civic responsibility up to ridicule. It insists that these walls, these lights are not part of a "school." In other words, it challenges the normalcy of UHS's physical and ideological structures. The conflicting messages convey double meanings, as does the sticker. Like the prisoner's Vaseline tube and the punk rocker's safety pin, it reflects legitimate and illegitimate uses. Hebdige states: "These humble objects can be magically appropriated; stolen by subordinate groups and made to carry secret meanings: meanings which express, in code, a form of resist-ance to the order which guarantees their continued subordination" (p. 18). In a space where teens assume a criminal stance, "stand straight for a few min-utes, legs apart . . . hands outstretched," tagging also reasserts a one-dimen-sional identity. It is a way that adolescent graffiti artists communicate to them-selves, to the guards, and to each other: I am here and I am potentially dan-gerous. Through tagging, students enter into a circular dynamic, some sort of violent exchange with both the institution and with each other.

> JENNIFER: What about the security guards? How do they interact
>   with you in the hallway?
> NIKKI: It all depends on what certain person it is. If someone is in
>   a gang or something like that, they'll watch you. They don't
>   really watch you that much.
> JENNIFER: How do they know if someone's in a gang?

NIKKI: It all depends, if they see your nametag up on the walls or
    stuff like that—and people call you by the name that's tagged
    up on the walls or someone just tells them.
JENNIFER: The kids put their names on the wall?
NIKKI: Yeah, all the stuff you see up on the hallway.

Like the language of a police log, the tag reduces individual complexity
by conveying a guise that appears to be unitary and continuous over time: "I
am and always will be dangerous." But naming moves away from complete
erasure; it captures the writer's presence, making him or her live, at least in
memory. Images that are scratched or marked on a wall allow us to go beyond
temporal constraints. This impulse to transcend time is eternal; it recalls ini-
tials carved into wooden desks, inscribed on pyramid tombs, marked on
Roman ruins. All who see such traces are reminded, paradoxically, of an
absence. Herein lies the tag's connection to texts that envision death.

A week after 17-year-old Ian Moore was shot in a Brooklyn high school,
the teen was eulogized at Community Baptist Church. During funeral serv-
ices, New York's mayor pledged millions of dollars for school security, and
1,000 mourners heard Moore's poetry.

> I fear death because I don't know
> what will happen when I go
> It is something I can't face
> When I die, will I be thought about?
> Will my name be shouted out?
> (Tabor, 1992, p. B3)

The poem moves from a simple acknowledgment, a declarative phrase,
to a series of ruminations: Will you remember me/Will I be resurrected? Like
speaking the names of the dead, tagging, like all writing, captures an image
that remains after the writer disappears. It allows him a measure of transcen-
dence. Too often, however, the tough pose and the tag simply lead to the bru-
talization of those who have nothing. Moreover, unlike poetry, the tag erases
the writer's complexity, and because it is confined to ravages of time and lim-
its of space, the tagger's influence, like his trace, is severely curtailed.

BEYOND MONOLITHIC LABELS

> Here was an arena, where I could be free—a place
> where I had the freedom to express myself. Poetry was

a small world within the larger world of school.
(Tanzania, December 10, 1998)

Poetry has the capacity to move students beyond a dehumanizing circular exchange (with the institution and each other), and in that place beyond, students are freer to slough off the restrictions of who they are, and discover parts of themselves long obscured by stigmatizing routines and simplistic tags. This freedom is inherently connected to form and process: what poetry allows (through brevity and opposition to a strict linear order) and what all expressive writing effects for the individual. Because of its potential to be non-narrative, or non-linear, a poet can engage confusion (chaos); she can watch it and write images discovered "amidst the substrata of preconscious feeling and intuition" (Poulin, 1991, p. 647). The poet does not necessarily create with intention.[1] She does not wield words, or gear them to a precise answer. Language may, in fact, subsume her, for poetry is a place where language has us at its disposition (Ricoeur, 1974, p. 93). The flux and indeterminacy of form allows non-rational experiences—the feelings of one's imaginative life—to enter consciousness. Paradoxically, poets use language to fend off chaos. Put metaphorically: "We are blind and poetry is the seeing eye dog that leads us around in the world."[2]

In the poem that follows, a piece I used to open this book, Tanzie constructs yet another shield, an aesthetic sanctuary, wherein her ability to control others emerges directly from the control she wields over her own visibility. This association is, of course, in conflict with the way she sees her body at the front door of her high school: "This is what I'm remembering when I had to stand in the position to scan me. The lady would scan me but there would be men right there looking and watching, making sure people get scanned. They're watching me get scanned. I'm standing like this [legs apart] and you're staring at me. I didn't like it." She transcends official categories, invisibility, and the penetration that accompanies criminal searches.

I am luna
I would rather be the moon than the sun
If I were the moon
I'd show just how much of me
I'd want everyone to see
If I am feeling particularly confident
I might just be a full moon
not ashamed
but ready to be seen and known and awed

If not very confident
or just particularly lazy
maybe just a crescent
or I might not show up at all
I am selene[3]
But when I'm full
and in charge
Look out!!!
Everyone just look out
Because I am in control
I control with my luminous beauty
I make you INSANE
I control the ocean
I pull the waves at my own will
and push them away when I'm through
I have control
More control than the sun

"I would rather be the moon than the sun." The writer's preference appears to stem from Luna's power to control her own visibility, to "show just how much of me I want everyone to see."

As Luna, Tanzania takes on a new sense of agency; she is a full moon, then a crescent, and finally a persona who pulls the waves at will and exerts more control than the sun. Early in the poem the writer establishes that her emotions determine appearance: when I am confident I am full; if lazy, just a crescent. Terms related to visibility are referenced throughout the text: "show just how much of me I'd want everyone to see," "I might just be a full moon . . . ready to be seen known and awed," "show up," "look out," "luminous beauty." Appearance is connected to being known and being awed, and it is connected to a kind of beauty that drives viewers mad.

The term "control" is repeated toward the end of the text, and every reference relates to the power of a full moon. In the end, Tanzania equates her desire to be Luna with an ability to control her viewers and nature itself. Her power is connected to a capacity to present herself at will: "When I am full moon and in charge, look out." Tanzania's readers never see a young woman stripped of all control over self-representation ("they are trying to take my shield away . . . [and] know my secrets"). With "I Am Luna," "they" see a mask, a manipulation of persona. Metaphor and personification unleash an imagination that defies the monolithic labels of the institution and the street. Through figurative language, Tanzie has transcended physical constraints, defining and redefining herself, despite the fixed definitions that limit her. In this context, poetry "embodies the principle of a free mind engaged in free action" (Kunitz, 1993, p. 17).

The writing exercises Hermine devised allowed students to go beyond the constraints implicit in all usual ways of thinking. "I have a tendency to push toward the unconscious." In doing so, she pushed them past flesh and blood—the sound of Subbie's voice, the feel of it—toward unverifiable things: dreams, fantasy, and perceptions of God. This realm was no less real for the writer than fact. In art (as in dreams), the test of reality does not come with the replication of material evidence. "For the point is not to copy something [in reality] but to reinvent it, reinvent it so that what is perceived actually feels true, and so that one can therefore believe in its continuance" (Dodd, 1992, pp. 119–120). The power of parallel worlds, of a reality so strong that one believes in its continuance, came to mind as I read the following story. On December 25, 2002, the musicians of the Iraqi National Symphony Orchestra were sitting down to play a Christmas concert when the electricity failed. Minutes passed before musicians lit candles near their scores and Emad Jamil, the tenor soloist, sang "Agnus Dei" from Bizet's *L'Arlesienne*. Later Jamil said, "We might as well have been playing in Bach's time. But at least I could forget myself in the music. For a short period of time, there was nothing but music" (MacFarquhar, 2002, p. A1). Perception, through our senses, grants us continuance, however brief.

Once Hermine asked her class "to imagine the place where God lives," and Nessa wrote "I See the World as Water." The reality of Nessa's perceptions provides her with a way out of dejection. In writing "I See the World as Water," she moves from mental oppression, a kind of psychic darkness, to renewed strength. Put metaphorically, she moves from constraint to fluidity.

> I see the world as water.
> Nice and blue and clean.
> The world should be like waves
> one after the other. My house
> is surrounded by water
> nobody to bother me. I live on
> an Island with God but nobody knows.
> It's in Jamaica.
> God is a black man who lives
> in Water. The Door to his house
> is always open for people who want

help. That's the World
Me and God live in.

In "I See the World as Water," Nessa redefines God and builds a parallel world around images of safety. When I asked her why she wrote the poem, she said that writing about God let her face loneliness:

When I wrote "I See the World as Water," I was feeling lonely—I didn't have as many people in my life then as I do now. I did not know if I would graduate from high school, so I wrote: 'The Door to his house is always open for people who want help,' and I believed God would always be there for me—that he would never leave me.

Nessa reinvents myths of heaven and earth, so that what she perceives *feels* true and this feeling of truth, of actuality, allows her to believe in the existence of a helpful God.

Earlier in the semester, Nessa had come to the tutoring room, and without much of a greeting, she began to tell me how she felt: "I have problems on my mind. Can't concentrate. Sometimes I feel like I have nobody. My mother's dead, my grandfather and my father, God only knows where he is."

JENNIFER: You have your aunt and your cousins.
NESSA: Yeah, I have my cousins.
JENNIFER: I remember you wrote about your aunt. That was a beautiful poem.
NESSA: Yeah, it's in the Hummingbird [poetry and prose journal].
JENNIFER: Would you like to write with me today? I'm taking a class with Hermine. Yesterday she asked us to write what was on our minds, thoughts about the day.

With little hesitation, she picks up a pen, but stops writing after a few moments. Her pen moves again. Then she stops for the last time.

JENNIFER: Do you want me to read it? [She moves the book in my direction, and I read:] "I'm not having a good day. I have problems on my mind." [The last sentence stretches across half a page. On a new line she writes,] "I am home." [But the sentence has been crossed out several times.]

JENNIFER: Why did you cross this out?
NESSA: I probably forgot what I wanted to say.

In her poem, "home" is not a stationary place but a quality within one-self, evoking dialogue and connection with God and others. "I See the World as Water" is a reinvention of the real world, one available through the senses and therefore seemingly true. As a reinvention, it became a way to see out-side loneliness, a way to get outside of it.

The image of water conveys security, a place where one will not be hurt; alien yet home. "Water is true to me, it is clean, it is pure." Water, pure and clean, surrounds home like a protective shield. In the last line, it becomes home, and Nessa lives in a shield, with God, in safety.

NOTES

1. Conversation with poet Julia Kasdorf.
2. Yehuda Amichai, an Israeli poet: Lecture at New York University, 1987. I would like to thank Julia Kasdorf for the reference.
3. Derived from "selenic," which means "of or pertaining to the moon" (Oxford English Dictionary, 1971, p. 2714).

CHAPTER 5

Conclusion

i watched them watch
i saw the same thing they saw
i watched the same thing they watched
why didn't i do anything?
—Tanzania

In June 1995, Tanzania and watched Nikki graduate from high school. We pulled up to the Brooklyn Academy of Music in a taxi. A crowd had gathered outside the entrance. Some vendors sell silver balloons with "Congratulations Class of '95" written in black. Others sell sashes with African patterns. "Class of '95" is woven into the cloth.

When we enter the auditorium, we are directed upstairs. The air is festive. People smile and wave; kids call out to each other. Eventually we take seats directly above the female graduates. They are clothed in white gowns. A guidance counselor begins the opening ceremony. After a brief welcome, he asks the graduates to stand and face their parents. Tanzania screams "There's Nikki!" "Where?" I ask. Then I see her. She stands facing the audience. She waves at someone I cannot see. Her smile seems bashful—it is not broad. But her eyes are direct. She is saying thank you with her smile, her eyes, her posture. Tanzie and I scream her name and she looks toward us. Her smile broadens. No longer humble. With her smile, she says, Good to see you.

The principal begins to speak to hushed crowd: "A week ago I attended my son's graduation. I thought that I couldn't be prouder. Today when I walked into the auditorium, I realized that I am equally proud of this class. You met the challenge, you the two hundred and fifty present. Those hundred who are not sitting with us did not meet the challenge." Tanzie looks around, and says, "I'm sad Nadia's not here." Nadia, the quiet girl who wrote gothic novels, does not graduate—at least, not today.

The ceremony lasts 2 hours and 45 minutes. Two hundred and fifty students get diplomas. Out of the 250 diplomas, 9 are college preparatory, or

New York State Regents' diplomas. Numerous awards are given; public corporations like Citibank confer several. Other awards are from religious groups. Serene (a young woman who struggles to read) gets an award for program completion.

TANZANIA: What program?
JENNIFER: I have no idea.

Students could not walk up to the stage fast enough. Counselors called each name and described each graduate's future plans. They could not read the information with enough speed. Before one degree was conferred, before a student reached the podium, another student would ascend the stairs. The names barely kept up with the bodies that moved across the stage. People screamed as several names were called. And Nikki danced toward her diploma. After the ceremony, students mingled in a foyer area away from the stage. One young man says hello to me. I do not recognize him. He says, "I've worked in this school for such a long time. Ran track, took night courses, and it's just this one math course. Can't graduate until I pass it." Serene emerges from a crowd of graduates and as she walks out the door, says, "Going to Kingsboro Community College. I'm going to be a nurse." The crowd of graduates, family, and friends move outside. I hand Nikki crushed flowers. She hugs me. "Nikki, you danced on the stage," I say. Her reply: "I wanted to make sure everyone saw me." She quickly moves off to a group of girls I have never seen. A boy talks to her. He wears a baseball cap, and looks older. People socialize for what seems like a long time. No one wants to leave. Nikki has a balloon in one hand and flowers in the other. After socializing myself, I approach her again. "'Bye Nikki, Class of '95." "Thank you," she says.

Between 1995 and 2004, I have spoken, or written, to Tanzania on a fairly regular basis (on average, once a month). She has completed 4 years of college. As part of her coursework, she returned to her former junior high school and taught creative writing to 120 eighth graders. She will receive a Masters in Education in the Spring of 2004, and plans to teach at the secondary level. When I spoke with Nikki in the fall of 1996, she wanted to leave her house, but had no job. She was babysitting for pocket money and thinking of becoming a teacher. Now she is studying to become a nurse. At age 19, Jhoy returned to St. Kitts; recent immigration laws prohibit her from remaining in New York with her mother and her older sister. A few months after she arrived on the island, she wrote "Exile," demonstrating the psychic tear that accompanies immigration—that perpetual longing for the other place. "I wrote 'Exile' a few months after I got back here. I missed New York and it felt like I was in exile. I couldn't go back until I had all the right papers, and I didn't want to stay here."

EXILE

"Oh stop it." I told myself in disgust.
I folded my coat around me
and held my coat tight to me, even though
I did not feel cold.

I missed him, but there was nothing
I could do about it.
I looked over the small channel
and looked at the island's lights.
Wishing they were the New York skyline.

Her return has been delayed by antiterrorist laws. Ironically, the immigrants who have worked to renew New York City by creating that sense of permanence, that connection to place, are now kept out.

Three years after Nikki danced toward her diploma, Nessa graduated from high school; she works at Macy's, sometimes 6 days a week. In the evening she comes home and cares for her nieces. "I don't go out much." Poetry has not provided her with financial security, and it never erased the time she spent in classrooms without books.

The complexity and the power of the writing completed at UHS has forced me to raise paradoxical questions about city schools. Urban High School did not promote academic rigor. As of this writing, it is slated for closure because it has low graduation rates, its 4-year graduation cohort is below 50%, and its students have "below standard" test scores. There is a danger, however, in dwelling too completely on academic failure—for this focus projects an image that easily veers off into sensationalism. Jeanne Theoharris convincingly writes:

> The crisis of urban education is invoked at once to damn black students, city schools, urban culture, public education and society in general—no matter the political persuasion, there seems to be general agreement that there is a crisis. Such lamentations give credence that, at some level, urban students are unreachable or unteachable. (Theoharris, 1996, p. 182)

Theoharris goes on to say "[T]his language of at-risk students and troubled schools" prevents us from seeing any joy in urban schools, and constructs Black children as the ultimate victims. Many students and teachers at UHS worked quietly and effectively on a daily basis. Young people attended theater workshops and tutoring sessions; teachers ran both. The school's steel drum band was one of the best, if not *the* best, in the city. Teens practiced after school on a weekly basis. On a personal level, I was more comfortable tutoring at UHS than in almost any other job. Young people brought me into their lives, into their intellectual and artistic work. I felt privileged.

Many UHS teachers worked hard and well with their students. When I asked Sara, a teacher who had developed a course in psychology on her own, to describe how she did her job, she replied:

> I read all the materials that I can get my hands on, books periodicals. I subscribe to about five different newsletters in health and mental health research, the Harvard Health Letter, the Berkeley Wellness Newsletter, a newsletter for social service workers in psychology, to make sure I know the latest research. I do weekly plans on Sunday when I sketch out all the topics and I make sure I know which articles I'm going to use. I sort of glean . . . My presentation always depends on my take of what's happening in the group.

Another teacher continually read books about the Caribbean and connected current events to the political history of his students' home countries. Kids seemed to trust him. They read aloud in his class, prompted by his gentle insistence. He once remarked, without a trace of condemnation, "Their reading reminds me of Freire's description of people who are just becoming literate: "They walk on the words." Good teachers are not unique. Mike Rose documents the ongoing work of city teachers in *Possible Lives: The Promise of Public Education in America.* He cites numerous examples of teachers who care about their students, hold out for academic rigor, and create "the conditions for children to develop lives of possibility" (Rose, 1995, p. 413). Despite these efforts, routines like scanning, the absence of resources, and overcrowded classrooms worked to obscure individual students: their histories, their fantasies, their dreams, and their interests.

In New York City the debilitation of comprehensive schools like UHS stems from long-term structural problems such as chronic teacher shortages and insufficient state funding. From 1997 to 1998, New York City educated nearly 38% of the state's students but received only 35.5% of the state education aid. State aid formulas do not necessarily offset local wealth.

Consequently, affluent districts can spend two to three times the amount spent by poor districts. The average per pupil expenditure in New York State from 1997 to 1998 was $10,342. New York City spent only $8,788 (Campaign for Fiscal Equity, 2000). In January 2001, New York State Supreme Court Judge Leland Degrasse found that New York State's financing formula was so biased that it violated the federal Civil Rights Act of 1964 by causing a disparate impact on Black and Latino children ("A Landmark School Ruling," 2001, p. A30). He stated: "The court holds that the education provided New York City students is so deficient that it falls below the constitutional floor set by the education article of the New York State Constitution" ("Excerpts from Judge's Ruling," 2001, p. B5). Degrasse went on to say that the labor needs of the city and state must be balanced with the needs of high school graduates. In other words, he argued that young people must be trained to move beyond service work so they are able to make a living wage. He eloquently argued, "Demography is not destiny. The amount of melanin in a student's skin, the home country of her antecedents, the amount of money in the family bank account, are not inexorable determinants of academic success" ("Excerpts from Judge's Ruling," 2001, p. B5). In June 2002, Degrasse's ruling was overturned by a state of appeals court. According to a panel of the appellate division of the Supreme Court, the state is only required to prepare students for the lowest-level jobs. Their interpretation of the state constitution emerged from their perception of what it means to function productively: "The ability to function productively should be interpreted as the ability to get a job, and support oneself and thereby not be a charge on the public fisc" (Justice Alfred J. Lerner, as cited in Perez-Pena, 2002, p. A1). The ruling helps replicate the labor needs of New York, but dismisses the needs of students in city schools. Given that a postindustrial economy has divided New York into two predominant groups, one affluent and the other unemployed or underemployed, "to function productively" can easily mean training for McDonalds.

When the appellate court's interpretation of the state constitution is considered alongside the gradual buildup of high-tech security tactics, we see the entrapment (or containment) of a Black population. This decision acts to preserve the historical disparity that Black children have experienced.[1] It calls into question the *public's* will to provide quality education for all students, and it counters the political rhetoric that culminated in the passage of "No Child Left Behind." Private companies are stepping in to fill the vacuum. In New York City, as in other large cities, they are funding ever larger public projects. The Carnegie Foundation, the Bill and Melinda Gates Foundation, and the Soros Foundation are behind efforts to restructure UHS and six other high schools in Central Brooklyn. When largesse replaces sustained public support, children in poor school districts become the recipients of charity; their rights under the state constitution are not debated—they are not even seen.

Teacher shortages in New York and other cities throughout the United States have led to the widespread hiring of an inexperienced staff that must work outside their fields of expertise. Meanwhile, teachers with seniority often leave the most overcrowded and dilapidated schools. This turnover engenders chaos. In the fall of 2001, 13 new teachers started teaching at an intermediate school near UHS—13 out of a teaching staff of 82. That year, students and staff also had to adjust to a new principal. Systemic reform has to include ways of attracting and keeping qualified personnel.

VIOLENCE IN SCHOOLS:
"YOU HAVE TO GO DEEPER TO CHANGE A PERSON"

> You can just size up whether a person will fight back
> by their appearance. You can tell by their appearance if
> they want to do it or not. I saw four boys beat the
> crap out of another boy on a city bus. At first when
> they hit him, he just sat there and when they contin-
> ued to hit him, he started hitting back. I started crying
> and said let me get off this bus. So I'm getting off the
> bus and the boy who was beaten got off the bus too.
> These kids sitting on a porch nearby came down and
> they're like "wow what happened to you?" He could-
> n't speak. Blood was all over the place. (Tanzania, May
> 1995)

The violence that initiated paramilitary security practices at UHS cannot be tolerated but it will not be stopped without public policies that address social problems. As O'Connor states,

> The simple truth is that the crisis in schools is not taking place only, or
> even primarily, in schools. It is also a crisis in health care and child care.
> It is the drug problem. It is child abuse, homelessness, racial and ethnic
> animosity, teenage motherhood. It is the scarcity of jobs, especially full-
> time jobs with decent pay and benefits. And, of course, it is violence.
> (O'Connor, 1993, p. 703)

Yet schools have some agency and some ability to effect change.

In the following conversation, Jhoy describes Nikki's response to another shooting.

> JENNIFER: Tell me what you remember about it [her poetry reading].
>
> JHOY: Umm. I think there were two poetry readings there. We had finished the posters. I went to the English department and gave these invitation flyers out. We told Ms. Walker and put invitations in the English teachers' mailboxes. Everyone teaching English that day let their class down. In one of them, Nikki came down. She was Ms. Walker's student for English. When she was reading, outside the library, in the street, someone shot a gun. And most of everybody dropped, some actually went to the window and this one fool ran out of the library into the hall and out the building to see what was going on. We thought he was crazy for going out there.
>
> JENNIFER: What did Nikki do?
>
> JHOY: She hid under the table. I don't know. I was looking outside. I just stopped, turned and saw a lot of people running. And Aresh told me she hid under the table.
>
> JENNIFER: What did you do?
>
> JHOY: I just stood there. Cause he wasn't aiming at the school. So I didn't think anything would happen to me.
>
> JENNIFER: Did you know it was gunfire?
>
> JHOY: I never heard one before, but I believed it was gunfire. And we heard screeches going down and then we heard police cars 'cause they're usually all around the school sometimes.
>
> JENNIFER: Hmmhmm.
>
> JHOY: That was fifth period. No one else showed up after that. It started from second period. During third, fourth, and fifth period there were a lot of people. After the gunshots, no one else showed up.

Jhoy's response begins with a poetry reading and ends in silence. "After the gunshots, no one else showed up." Nikki and the teachers who brought their students to the reading are shoved down or pushed out to the periphery—completely disrupted by gunfire and the sound of police cars. These actors must be the central players in any plan that promotes safety.

Pedro Noguera argues, "[T]he preoccupation with controlling student behavior has inadvertently weakened the school's ability to ensure safety" (Noguera, 1999). He insists that schools listen to students and teachers, and to their fears. Four years after she graduated from high school, Tanzania explained student-teacher interaction as follows: "It's hard for them to police and teach—all students were treated harshly. You can't seem soft, if a potential criminal is ready to pounce." In my conversations with UHS students, many acknowledged the futility of the school's security practices.

> Students sneak bottles into school. They put razors in their mouths and walk through scanners. You have to go deeper to change a person. Scanners won't do it. (Eva, a student at UHS)

Students and teachers believe that personal contact between adults and teens reduces violence (Noguera, 1999). Hermine Meinhard's workshops reflected that contact: "The structure of the group contained a situation; trust emerges." When she started working at UHS, Hermine was placed in a class of students who had been characterized as slow learners. Their English teacher had told her that it was nearly impossible to engage them in discussion, and that most of his classwork involved guided reading. In her notes that semester, she wrote, "It quickly became clear to me that these students where not slow, they were angry. They had a great deal to say and the workshops gave them an opportunity to say it." Twenty students attended her class regularly. They sat around the perimeter of the room, against the wall. To get closer, Hermine went into the middle of the room. She taught her third lesson on the day of the Los Angeles riots. Students were angry, seemingly distracted, but they wrote with absorption. Hermine said, "I told them to write everything that was in their hearts and minds about the riots, opening with 'I have something to say and you will listen'."

During the fifth class, she worked with repetition. After writing a collaborative poem, she asked students to write individually. Ken did not pick up a pen. He told Hermine he could not think of a phrase to use. She suggested "What the hell," and he smiled.

> What the hell!
> What people take us
> Hard working People
> for. We always
> trying to make the world the best place
> there is to me the

world is blue has
the full blue
of the sea.
I do give some thanks
some people that trying
to make the world free
from trouble, racism
and crime. I'm not
racist but I'm curious
about the future of
my people and my
family. What the
hell they take
us for. What they
Really, Really take us
for.

Ken wields the line—what the hell—to point his anger. But perhaps more important than grasping the power of repetition and honing his literary voice is the opportunity to express a vision. Kenneth saw, and told his audience, that the world has the full blue of the sea, and he gave thanks. What resounds in the work is his concern for others, his family, and his people. When Hermine read the poem at the beginning of the following class, Darren, a teenager who usually kept his head on his desk, turned to Ken and said, "You wrote that?"

Teaching English Education at Brooklyn College, I have met high school English teachers whose students write poetry outside of school. Like Tanzania, they jot it down in big, messy notebooks, reminding their teachers "how difficult it is to remain just one person." (Milosz, "Ars Poetica"). For teenagers living in the poorest neighborhoods of New York City, the persona of the poet allows them to temporarily drop a tough pose and become vulnerable. I quote April Leong, a young woman who teaches in Brownsville, New York, at length in order to convey how her students confront the threat of violence:

The majority of my students act as if they are immune to losing people close to them and they themselves take death in stride. "I don't care if I die today, you have to go some day," seems to be the most popular attitude taken by both males and females. Getting to see another day alive is like the draw of the lottery to some and these are the some who do not hold the lives of others in high regard. "It's either him or me, so if I got to get him first, the so be it." It's a popular defense for the males who are willing to take someone else's life. They want to come across as tough and unaffected by death, but usually it is just a front.

Later she wrote about one student who temporarily loses the front and acknowledges his desire to remain attached to others.

> Anton's uncle is ill and two friends of his friends were just murdered. Both murders were gang related. Anton says he knows his day is coming up and wishes someone would take him out soon because he is tired of watching people around him die. In the midst of the conversation, he mentions a couple of students who need to watch their steps. "They are lucky I am in control today," he says with a smirk. Just then he decides to share his secret hobby with me. He takes out his notebook of poetry. Anton has twelve poems he has written about the love of his life and the young son he wants to give to the world.

The notebook becomes Anton's asylum, an emotional preserve made up of multiple dreams that make him care about the world and the people in it. And while in that asylum he dropped his smirk, his disdain, and forgot the pain that catches him, causing him to court death. Writing thus prevented the dynamics of a throw-away society. Anton's poetry, his notebook—with its 12 poems—and the school where he and April interact are sites of preservation. They are sacred. While he is writing, and while he is speaking to April, Anton does not throw away stable relationships, attachments to people. Rather, he lingers over those connections, over "the love of his life and the son he wants to give to the world."

Writing poetry may not have stopped violence, but it reinforced expressions of humanity. Imagination led to empathy; it allowed students to transcend their own lives in order to visualize what life was like for others. Tanzania wrote "Christine" after she saw a red mark on a classmate's face.

CHRISTINE!

Small girl
quiet girl
with a small

and quiet
voice.
You scare me,
my dear.
I never
knew you
or
cared of you,
until the day I met your mother.
Nice lady.
Concerned
for her small and
quiet daughter.
Christine!
I am so sorry I spoke
too soon.
Telling her I knew not
of
your whereabouts.
I thought she was just concerned.
but I knew
it was more than concern
when I saw
your red bruised face
the next day.
She's followed
you to where
she is not
and watched.
She's just making sure you stay the way
she wants you.
Do you see it too?

After writing the poem, she said: "I thought that by watching, I could stop whatever was happening, watching was like doing something physical." In this instance, writing and relationship interface, each enhancing the quality of the other. Concern for another human being seems to reinforce Tanzania's belief that her perceptions are worth telling, and writing solidifies her concern for Christine. Furthermore, by witnessing abuse and subsequently writing about it, Tanzania moves from personal alarm to collective responsibility. By watching, Tanzania holds herself responsible for someone else. By writing, she holds us responsible.

Poetry was an act of appropriation. Words became weapons, as young people used them to their own ends. Some made great poems out of the experience of seeing violent acts. Their works were affirmations of survival, expressions of dreams, and visions of the world which connected them, so beautifully, to it, to the "deep full blue of the sea."

INTERNALIZING A GUIDING VOICE IN SCHOOL

you, holding this thing up to me
                    fractures   the way I always was
—Hermine Meinhard, "Teacher"

Nikki, Nessa, Jhoy, and Tanzania saw too many shootings during their 4 years at UHS—and they sat in too many classrooms where teachers "passed you for the hell of it." Yet their imaginations were not constrained by social circumstances and it is that imagination that we, as teachers, must continue to celebrate, cultivate, and in all circumstances, defend.

On September 9, 1999, 8 years after I began tutoring at UHS, the New York City Board of Education ended Social Promotion, a policy that moved students from grade to grade regardless of their attendance or academic performance. All high school students must now have a certain number of credits to be promoted, and they must pass Regents exams to graduate. Those who fail are sent to summer school. State governors from around the country are engaged in bidding wars to attract qualified teachers to low-performing schools. After years of silence regarding the systemic neglect of city schools, the *New York Times* noted that these bidding wars do not address the salary imbalances that put these schools at a disadvantage with relation to the state's suburbs. The city raised teacher salaries in June 2002. Clearly this attention and the measures that have emerged from it begin to address the academic neglect I have documented in this book.

New York's attempt to confront social promotion and attract teachers is part of a nationwide effort to raise academic standards. As part of that effort, we have seen a push to establish norms that are easily tested. The trend brings us back to a focus on individual achievement. Testing completely shifts responsibility for success to individual teachers and students rather than placing it on city and state politicians. Thus it does not hold public officials accountable for years of civic neglect. In New York, the print media have reinforced an emphasis on individual success (or failure), touting headlines like "Math Test Disaster 77% Flunk New 8th-Grade State Exam, 19 More Schools Flunk; But 13 Improve Enough to Escape Hall of Shame." Shaming students and teachers undermines any public discussion about why schools have failed a population that is predominantly Black and Latino and almost exclusively working class and poor. It also fails to link systemic failure to an ideology of containment, or to any discussion regarding the link between school and economy. In her analysis of the Chicago School Reform, Pauline Lipman explains the current embrace of standardized testing as a desire for simplistic, technical solutions—a desire that ultimately prevents a public analysis of historically rooted problems (Lipman, 1999). She contends that schools serving low-income children of color have implemented test-driven, scripted education, while magnet schools develop intellectually rigorous curricula. Constant reminders of standards are ubiquitous in schools educating students who represent a low-wage section of the labor force. Lipman surmises that the intensified boredom and regimentation endemic to this kind of education may "weed out" any teenager who is superfluous (and potentially dangerous) to the postindustrial city.

As it has in Chicago, the scripted education dictated by New York's Standards Movement has reinforced the inequity of a multitiered school system. For a journal assignment in one of my education courses at Brooklyn College, one student noted the following differences between a neighborhood middle school in Bedford-Stuyvesant, a neighborhood that is African American and poor, and an integrated alternative school in Downtown Manhattan.

> Teaching, learning, and assessment at [the Bedford-Stuyvesant school] is based on a rubric system. In this system, a student receives a number grade. I remember there was a specific rubric for reading that was written on the chalkboard in the resource room—next to each number was a description of a skill the student had to grasp. The reading teacher returned papers with small red numbers on the top corner of a student's work. No written comments. I observed the same grading process in the social studies class. At [the Downtown Manhattan school] instructors did not assign a numerical grade. They wrote progress reports 2–4 times per semester. Rather than a grade, the report provided an in-depth discus-

sion of a student's progress: his strengths and weaknesses. While observing, I asked a student if I could see a typed paper recently returned to her. It was ungraded but filled with comments, suggestions, criticisms. (Moza Mfuni, May, 2001)

Another student wrote: "The teachers at [the Bedford-Stuyvesant School] felt the Board of Education imposed, to an unnecessary extent, how they taught, and what they taught. The consensus was that they were stifled by a system that does not know its students." Both of my undergraduates described the teachers from Bedford-Stuyvesant as hard-working people who spent their own money on school supplies, but whose efforts were undermined by a bureaucratic system that "stifled" teaching. Paperwork, standards, and rubrics frequently prevented teachers from seeing individual students. The collective script undermined the desire embedded in "Teacher," Hermine's poem: the (un)likelihood that students would ever "internalize a guiding voice that helps them claim parts of themselves."

Lipman suggests, and numerous educators have argued, that we promote both basic and critical literacy by developing curricula that give students opportunities to use their own reality as a basis for literacy (Lipman, 1999). Before she left UHS, Hermine planned a series of exercises that linked creative and analytical writing. She wanted her students to build an argument based totally on the experiences of their senses. Reason had already found its way into Nessa's understanding of her place within a social hierarchy: "They don't like me. Why? Because I'm different from them. I come from a poor family." Through a detailed description of rape, reason had found its way into Tanzie's analysis of racism. And into one young man's understanding of his mother's material existence and her rage: "Works for the men, I hate those shitheads. And in us she sees the men, the men we become." By asking students to attend to what they saw and what they heard, by making them responsible for detail, Hermine pushed them toward reason. By consciously coupling reason and perception, she may have pushed them further toward a critical analysis of their lives. Perhaps this makes her suspect. As Robert Scholes writes: "What this society does not want from its educational institutions is a group of people imbued with critical skills and values that are frankly agonistic to those that prevail in our marketplaces, courts, and our legislative bodies" (Scholes, 1998, p. 19). However, Scholes's belief about society erases, or at least reduces, the multiple and contradictory desires of individual teachers.

The poetry that Nikki, Tanzania, Nessa, and Jhoy wrote conveyed a complex representation of self and world that came from their senses and from unverifiable desire. By writing, they recorded material reality and consciously changed it. Both the record and the alteration are evident in the following stories, and both stories tell us that what matters to students are the lives of those around them—brothers, friends, neighbors, family—people they care about and often love. Writing begins with images steeped in an oppressive reality but it leads to perceptions of what could be. Tanzania and Nikki write about physical transformations for themselves and for others. Their imagination was thus a powerful social force.

I once showed Tanzania the transcript of a taped conversation in which she equated poetry with the freedom of expression. She told me a story I had heard before.

> JENNIFER: You said, "Here was a place where I had the freedom to express myself." Does poetry provide that freedom? Does Meinhard provide it?
>
> TANZANIA: When you ask me that question, I remember being in the car with my father and seeing men shooting at each other. I was telling on them. I believe, I was telling God. [Seconds of silence.] When I wrote about these shootings, I also remember thinking, no one's writing about it. No one's written about it.

Tanzie not only relies on her own reality as the basis for literacy, as Lipman advocates; she relies on it as the basis for social analysis and spiritual expression. Her concern for her neighborhood, for Black men, stands in direct opposition to Justice Learner's interpretation of New York State's constitution—"to get a job and support oneself and thereby not be a charge on the public fisc." It stands in opposition to the notion that we can throw away people and places. The act of witnessing fuels a desire to transform what she sees—in itself, it is an act of refusal. When she writes to tell on people, she imagines that social transformation is possible. She associates freedom with her belief in transformation. Consequently, "The place where I had the freedom to express myself" is not Hermine's workshops; it is not expression itself; freedom emerges from her own conception of what should be, and writing is her vehicle to transform what is.

The next story begins with Nikki. Once she once came into the tutoring room during her lunch hour. She seemed restless, and I remember working hard in order to get her to focus. As we talked, students ate lunch; discarded milk cartons and books lay on tables. The room was messy but five tutors and roughly 25 students worked and ate quietly. Nikki was disturbing the peace. I asked her to write, and suggested she begin with a line that I would provide. I had worked with Hermine in this way. She would "throw" language—lines from novels, published poems, and newspaper articles. Sometimes she told her students to use the line three times, and sometimes she simply told them to keep it in the back of their minds. Nikki was familiar with the technique and readily asked me for a line.

> JENNIFER: "I have something to say, and you will listen."
> NIKKI: No.
> JENNIFER: "What the hell."
> NIKKI: No.
> JENNIFER: "Here I am."
> NIKKI: No.

I looked at local headlines, made sentences out of phrases. She rejected five or six lines before I told her I had run out of ideas. "You have to do what Miss Meinhard does. Take objects, move them around, or ask me to move them around, and I'll imagine a scene." I looked down the long wooden table where we sat, and saw nothing. I could work spontaneously with words, but I had to think about an object's symbolism in advance. As we sat, I imagined myself in the East Village buying dried flowers. "I have to shop for something," I said. "I'll bring in fruit or flowers or masks." "You don't have to shop for anything. Take this," Nikki said. She grabbed a salt shaker and a cardboard box. Then she wrote about a sick baby girl who lay in a hospital incubator. The mother in Nikki's poem watches her baby through the plated glass of a hospital window and imagines a dancer.

Nikki took a salt shaker and cardboard box in order to write. Her insistence on method, on the way to structure an exercise, tells us that teaching and learning can be spontaneous, that they can be dialogic; and that when they are done well, students internalize both the teacher and student role. The story tells us that young people can choose material through which they find their individuality. It also tells us that invention, through language, is limited by nothing but our own ingenuity. But this focus on teaching and individuality does not address the specifics of the poem: the family, the hospital corridors, the sick child. The work's content bears a striking resemblance to a poem written by her friend, Andre, a young man who stayed in touch with her for years.

The year before Nikki wrote her poem, she and Andre sat in Hermine's class and responded to an exercise that emphasized the specificity of place. They drew pictures of places that were important to them: rooms, churches, playgrounds. They drew the shape of these places and everything in them, and they listed things—namely, combs, telephones, flowers, trees, posters, and people. Then they followed Hermine's final request: "Write a piece in any form you want, starting with, "When I got there, everything had changed." And Andre wrote:

WHEN I GOT THERE EVERYTHING HAD CHANGED

First of all my son is not with me, he is in the hospital.
The palm trees are gone.
The whole place seems barren. Sort of plain.
No longer are we having fun. Instead
I am standing over his hospital bed
Praying that he will be alright.

I see Nikki's work as a desire to go back to Andre, to see him, to empathize with him. I also see, in its symbolism, the power of poetry itself: to take what is and imagine what is possible.

THE PURPOSE OF POETRY

If schools are sacred places, they must become sites of preservation; they must grasp the democratic spirit of a graduation pledge, repeated over generations—I pledge to obey my country's laws, according to my conscience—and they must preserve the writing that comes out of life: rhythms of the pulpit (or the Jamaican market); Subbie's voice; and Kerry's grandfather stories.

Like so many great American poets, UHS students wrote from experience and they wrote well. They, in turn, gained wisdom by wielding metaphor and detailing imagery. In fact, I would go as far as Muriel Rukeyser did when she said that writing poetry equipped the imagination to deal with life itself (Rukeyser, 1994, p. 121), and I would add that it allows a measure of transcendence, for Nessa's voice still resonates: "When I wrote 'I See the World as Water' I was feeling lonely. . . . I did not know if I would graduate from high school, so I wrote, 'The door to his house is always open for people who want to help.'" For Nessa, Nikki, Andre, and others, poetry became "a scream in the night, an emancipation of language and old ways of thinking" (Kelley, 2002, p. 58).

For the past several years, Peter Taubman and I have organized Day of the Poet, a poetry festival that invites high school students from the borough of Brooklyn to hear published poets read and to write poetry themselves. The event occurs at Brooklyn College. Denis Nurkse, one of the event's workshop leaders once told me: "We want to get kids out of high schools, where they do not necessarily have reputations as poets, and to a college where their creativity is celebrated." In December 2001, we asked students to read their own work for the first time in the Day of the Poet's history. I sat on stage with quiet kids, many seemingly shy, some visibly nervous and unsure of themselves. One said, "Miss, I can't read." "Sure you can," I said. "Well, can I say this?" A skinny girl pointed to the word "penis." I said, "Say it." I called one name, then another. "Jorge Ramos." A short, young man, walked to the podium. He, too, seemed a bit shy, holding my glance ever so briefly, as if to say, "Can I?" or "Thank you." And then looked away.

Ramos was short and heavy—he moved slowly, awkwardly, his weight threw him off balance. He seemed to shift into the mike. "My name is Jalapeno. My friends have heard the next poem so many times, I'm afraid they will be a bit bored. Sorry."

He began a slam, holding his voice steady, then raising it. "I write the words." He spoke of bleeding words, bleeding *Webster's Dictionary*, he punned; he brought his hand down suddenly, moved his body in performance. When he stopped, every student was on his or her feet, yelling and clapping. A skinny girl who had been sitting on stage, waiting to read, stood up and screamed "I write the words, too!" Jalapeno was no longer the kid who walked awkwardly to a mike. Everyone in that audience saw a poet, a young man who brought a crowd to its feet and inspired a young woman to scream his words.

Margaret Watts, another workshop leader, gave me a more intimate account of the ways students recognize each other.

> Have I told you what happened in my poetry workshop? I had a gang member who did none of my morning exercises. Then, after lunch, he wrote a poem about a friend who was shot by the police, rushed to the hospital, and died when he was given the wrong blood. When he read that poem, you could have heard a pin drop. Later in the day, someone else in the group, a young woman, responded to his poem with a poem of her own.

The poem, "Lament for Brothers," was a testament to one teen's ability to create something beautiful after listening to a stranger's horrific experience. And by listening, she leaves herself open to grief, and to think about the heart-wrenching possibilities of what could have been had a young Black man lived.

"Lament for Brothers" is reminiscent of war-time laments or eulogies, written by women who watch their sons leave for battle. More recently,

women of color, women who have lost men to the violence perpetrated by
gangs or by the police, have read memorial poems in public; their dead
becoming "invisible guests," who come in and out of their dreams at will.
In a tribute to Amadou Diallo, a West-African man shot and killed by New
York City police on February 4, 1998, Angeli Rasbury told an audience,
"This is one way of surviving" ("At Poets' Gathering," 2000, p. B6).
Mourning may access a collective consciousness, raising words that are
archetypal, specific to a people's existence. The third stanza of Audre
Lorde's "Eulogy for Alvin Frost" resonates with the young woman's
imagery.

> I am tired of writing memorials to black men
> whom I was on the brink of knowing
> weary like fig trees
> weighted like a crepe myrtle
> with all the black substance poured into earth
> before earth is ready to bear.

Trees rooted but weighted by mourning appear in both texts. Later in
"Eulogy," Lorde urges Alvin Frost's son to grown up "black and strong and
beautiful," and then ends the last line of her poem with a refrain that echoes
the unifying thread in "Lament": "but not too soon."

In the final lines of her poem "They Saw," Tanzie holds herself respon-
sible for social powerlessness—single-handedly shouldering a heavy load.
Yet by writing, she allows others to witness "what is happening," and as
witnesses we, too, must choose whether to act. By writing she connects
with others, distributes responsibility, and fosters the hope of a collective
consciousness.

THEY SAW

> they saw
> i know they saw
> sleepy eyes saw
> i saw sleepy eyes see
> i watched the sleepy eyes widen with horror
> they saw
> i saw them see it happen
> i saw them acknowledge the morbid picture
> so why didn't they do anything

when they know they saw
i know they saw it happen
i saw them seeing it
they didn't stop it
they just watched
i watched them watch
i saw the same thing they saw
i watched the same thing they watched
why didn't i do anything?

Five years after Nessa and Tanzania were in Meinhard's class, I met them on a Manhattan street. We went to dinner and Tanzie talked about a poetry reading Hermine had scheduled at a local university. I turned to Nessa and said, "Your entire family showed up—Subbie, your uncle, and all your cousins."

NESSA: Yeah, I had forgotten about that.
JENNIFER: What made you come to the poetry workshops, initially?
NESSA: I felt important.
JENNIFER: You felt important when you read?
NESSA: I felt important during the whole thing. I was happy to be
    a part of it.

The poetry workshops that Hermine initiated opened up public places where human beings came together in their freedom, and entered into dialogue with one another as *who* and not *what* they are (Greene, 1998). Tanzania has continued to open *public* places where students revisit their lives and interact as *who* they are. After returning to her former junior high school to teach poetry, she told me:

I'd write back to the students and they'd get all giddy. I don't think
they were used to teachers writing to them. One boy said, "Look, you
drew a girl on my paper." I said, "Yeah, and she's talking to you."

NOTE

1. On June 27, 2003, nearly 50 years after the Brown v. Board of Education decision, New York State's Court of Appeals reversed the appellate court's ruling, acknowledging that functioning in this society entails a high school education.

References

Abu-Lughod, L. (1991). Writing against culture. In R. G. Fox (Ed.), *Recapturing anthropology* (pp. 137–162). Santa Fe, NM: School of American Research Press.

Althusser, L. (1971). *Lenin and philosophy: And other essays.* New York: Monthly Review Press.

Angelo, L. (1995). Marching to its own drummer: Why wage trends in New York have diverged. *Urban Affairs Review, 31*(1), 104–120.

Anyon, J. (1997). *Ghetto schooling: A political economy of urban educational reform.* New York: Teachers College Press.

Apple, M. (1983). Curricular form and the logic of technical control. In M. Apple & L. Weis (Eds.), *Ideology and practice in schooling.* Philadelphia: Temple University Press.

Apple, M. & Weis, L. (1983). *Ideology and practice in schooling.* Philadelphia: Temple University Press.

Applebome, P. (1997, April 8). Schools see re-emergence of "separate but equal": Desegregation efforts ending, study finds. *The New York Times,* pp. A8, A10.

Archibold, R. (1999, September 9). Over one member's objection, Board ends social promotion. *The New York Times,* p B4.

Arsenault, W. [District Attorney of New York City] (1997, November 12). An overview of Manhattan gangs. Schools and Safety: Theory and Praxis Collogium Series at New York University.

Bakhtin, M. (1994). The dialogic imagination: Four essays. In P. Morris (Ed.), *The Bakhtin reader: Selected writings of Bakhtin, Medvedev, Voloshinov* (pp. 25–87). London: Edward Arnold.

Behar, R. (1995). Rage and redemption: Reading the life story of a Mexican marketing woman. In D. Tedlock & B. Mannheim (Eds.), *The dialogic emergence of culture* (pp. 148–178). Urbana and Chicago: University of Illinois Press.

Berger, J. (1992, March 5). Teachers union, in solid front, authorizes walk-outs. *The New York Times,* p. B4.

Bourgois, P. I. (1995). *In search of respect: Selling crack in El Barrio.* Cambridge, UK: Cambridge University Press.

Brace, C. L. (1880). *The dangerous classes, and twenty years work among them.* New York: Wynkoop & Hallenbeck Publishers.

Bracken, C. (1992). Coercive spaces and spatial coercions: Althusser and Foucault. *Philosophy & Social Criticism, 17*(3), 229–241.

Brown, M. K. (1991). *Moma Lola: A vodou priestess in Brooklyn.* Berkeley: University of California Press.

Buck-Morss, S. (1989). *The dialectics of seeing: Walter Benjamin and the arcades project.* Cambridge, MA: MIT Press.

Callahan, R. (1962). *Education and the cult of efficiency.* Chicago: University of Chicago Press.

Campaign for Fiscal Equity. (2000, November). *In evidence: Policy reports from the CFE trial: Vol. 2.* New York: Author.

Chadwick, B. (1982, August 17). Job world is learned by students. *Daily News,* p. K11.

Citizens Committee for Children of New York. (1995). *Keeping track of New York's children.* New York: Author.

Clifford, J. (1988). *The predicament of culture: Twentieth century ethnography, literature and art.* Cambridge, MA: Harvard University Press.

Cremin, L. A. (1988). *American education: The metropolitan experience 1876–1980.* New York: Harper & Row.

Crown Heights Coalition. (1992). *Crown Heights: A strategy for the future: A report of the Crown Heights Coalition prepared in cooperation with the Brooklyn borough president.* New York: Author.

Damon, M. (1993). *The dark end of the street.* Minneapolis: University of Minnesota Press.

Davis, M. (1992). *City of quartz: Excavating the future in Los Angeles.* New York: Vintage.

Denton, N. A., & Massey, D. S. (1993). *American apartheid: Segregation and the making of the underclass.* Cambridge, MA: Harvard University Press.

Devine, J. (1990). *Blackboard jungle revisited: The semiotics of violence in an urban school.* Unpublished doctoral dissertation, New York University

Devine, J. (1995). Can metal Detectors replace the panopticon? *Cultural Anthropology, 10*(2), 171–195.

Devine, J. (1996). *Maximum security: The culture of violence in inner-city schools.* Chicago: University of Chicago Press.

Dillon, S. (1993a, December 24). On the barricades against violence in the schools. *The New York Times,* p. B1.

Dillon, S. (1993b, December 5). Security system is failing tests in high schools. *The New York Times,* p. A1.

Dillon, S. (1994, September 21). Cortines wants 50 high schools to get walk-through detectors. *The New York Times*, p. B3.

Dodd, W. (1992). *Toward the end of the century: Essays into poetry.* Iowa City: University of Iowa Press.

Dreyfus, H., & Rabinow, P. (1982). *Michel Foucault: Beyond structuralism and hermeneutics.* Chicago: University of Chicago Press.

Eagle Staff Photo. (1948, January 31). *The Brooklyn Eagle*, p. 3.

Educational Video Center (Producer/Director). (1993). *360 degrees of violence.* [Videocassette]. (Available from the Educational Video Center, 55 East 25th Street, Suite 407, New York, NY, 10010)

Elbow, P. (2000). *Everyone can write: Essays toward a hopeful theory of writing and teaching writing.* New York: Oxford University Press.

English, M. (1987, July 19). Crown Heights: Harassment or desperation?: Blacks, Hassidim agree all lose in hunt for housing. *New York Newsday*, pp. 6, 28.

Excerpts from judge's ruling on school financing. (2001, January 11). *The New York Times*, p. B5.

Feldman, A. (1991). *Formations of violence.* Chicago: University of Chicago Press.

Firestone, D. (1995, August 23). Giuliani criticizes a U.S. crackdown on illegal aliens. *The New York Times*, p. B6.

Ford Foundation. (1993). *Changing relations—newcomers and established residents in US communities.* New York: Author.

Foucault, M. (1977a). Nietzsche, genealogy, history. In D. F. Bouchard (Ed.), *Michel Foucault: Language, counter memory, practice: Selected essays and interviews* (pp. 139–164). New York: Cornell University Press.

Foucault, M. (1977b). Revolutionary action: Until now. In D. F Bouchard (Ed), *Michel Foucault: Language, counter memory, practice: Selected essays and interviews* (pp. 218–233). New York: Cornell University Press.

Foucault, M. (1979). *Discipline and punish.* New York: Vintage Books.

Foucault, M. (1982). The Subject and power. In H. Dreyfus & P. Rabinow (Eds.), *Michel Foucault: Beyond structuralism and hermeneutics* (pp. 208–226). Chicago: University of Chicago Press.

Fresco, R. (2001, March 16). Census 2000; and the numbers are in; New York population grows by 1 million; metropolitan area increases in diversity. *New York Newsday*, p. E02.

Freud, S. (1998). *The interpretation of dreams.* (J. Strachey, Trans.). New York: Avon. (Original work published 1900)

Frye, N. (1976). *The secular scripture: A study of the structure of romance.* Cambridge, MA: Harvard University Press.

Frye, N. (1985). Approaching the lyric. In C. Hosek & P. Parker (Eds.), *Lyric poetry: Beyond new criticism* (pp. 31–37). Ithaca, NY: Cornell University Press.

George, N. (1998). *hip hop america.* New York: Penguin Books.

Gest, T. (1995). A shocking look at Blacks and crime. (Sentencing project's report on African-American prison inmates). *U.S. News and World Report, 119*(15), 53–55.

Glass, D., Orfield, G., Reardon, S., & Schley, S. (1994). The growth of segregation in American schools: Changing patterns of separation and poverty since 1968. *Equity & Excellence in Education, 27*(1), 5–9.

Godfrey, B. J. (1995). Restructuring and decentralization in a world city. *The Geographical Review, 85*(4), 436–458.

Goffman, E. (1959). *The presentations of self in everyday life.* New York: Doubleday.

Goffman, E. (1961). *Asylums: Essays on the social situation of mental patients and other inmates.* Chicago: Adeline Publishing.

Greene, M. (1998, July 14). Imagination and perception. Lincoln Center Institute [online]. Retrieved November 5, 2001. Available: www.lcinstitute.org.

Harris, N. (1995). *The new untouchables: Immigration and the new world worker.* London: Penguin Books.

Hartocollis, A. (2001, March 22). Not-so-simple reasons for drop-out rate. *The New York Times*, p. B6.

Harvey, D. (1989). *The condition of postmodernity.* Oxford, UK: Basil Blackwell.

Hebdige, D. (1988). *Subculture: The meaning of style.* London and New York: Routledge.

Hemphill, C., & Whitaker, B. (1988, July 12). This streetcart named Desire: Vendors push midtown protest. *New York Newsday*, pp. 3, 31.

Hobsbawm, E. (2003, July 4). Only in America. *The Chronicle of Higher Education* [online]. Retrieved July 11, 2003. Available: http://chronicle.com/free/v49/ i43/43b00701.htm

Jameson, F. (1984). Postmodernism, or the cultural logic of late capitalism. *New Left Review, 146*, 53–92.

Kappstatter, R. (1971, July 30). Blockbusting curb is upheld by the court. *Daily News*, p. 15.

Kappstatter, R. (1977, February 14). Teachers threaten job action in student violence. *Daily News*, p. K4.

Kelley, R. (1994). *Race rebels: Culture, politics and the Black working class.* New York: Free Press.

Kelley, R.D.G. (2002). Beyond the "real" world: Or why black radicals need to wake up and start dreaming. *Souls: A Critical Journal of Black Politics, Culture, and Society, 4*(2), 51–64.

Kunitz, S. (1993). *Interviews and encounters with Stanly Kunitz.* New York: Sheep Meadow Press.

A Landmark School Ruling, (2001, January 11). *The New York Times,* p. A30.

Limón, J. (1994). *Dancing with the devil: Society and cultural poetics in Mexican American South Texas.* Madison: University of Wisconsin Press.

Lipman, P. (1999, November). *Chicago school policy and the cultural politics of race.* Paper presented at the annual meeting of the American Anthropological Association, Chicago.

Loetterle, F. (1970, April 27). Crown Heights is fighting not to become a slum. *Daily News,* p. 6.

Lorde, A. (1984). *Sister outsider.* New York: Crossing Press.

Lorde, A. (1986). *Our dead behind us.* New York: W. W. Norton.

Lorde, A. (1992). *Undersong: Chosen poems old and new.* New York: W. W. Norton.

Lucas, P. (1995). *Violent passages: An ethnographic study on the experience of space, place, and time in a public high school.* Unpublished doctoral dissertation, New York University.

Macdonell, D. (1986). *Theories of discourse: An introduction.* Cambridge, MA: Basil Blackwell.

MacFarquhar, N. (2002, December 26). Threats and responses: Life in Iraq. *The New York Times,* p. A1.

Massey, D., & Denton, N. (1993). *American Apartheid: Segregation and the making of the underclass.* Boston: Harvard University Press.

McCallister, J. (1985, October 3). Pepsi generation gets firm's support. *Daily News,* p. K8.

Medoff, P., & Sklar, H. (1994). *Streets of hope: The fall and rise of an urban neighborhood.* Boston: South End Press.

Mitchell, A. (1995, February 15). Giuliani transformed. *The New York Times,* p. B5.

Mitchell, S. (2001, November/December). Letter to a young writer. *Teachers & Writers, 33*(2), 25–27.

Myers, S. L. (1995, June 11). In budget battle between mayor and the council, the devil is in the details. *The New York Times,* p. B45.

New York City Board of Education. (1922). *Pupils' progress through the grades.* New York: Author.

New York City Department of City Planning. (1992). *The newest New Yorkers: An analysis of immigration into New York City during the 1980s.* New York: Author.

New York City Department of City Planning. (1993). *Socioeconomic profiles: A portrait of New York City's community districts from the 1980 & 1990 censuses of population and housing.* New York: Author.

New York City Department of City Planning. (1996). *The newest New Yorkers, 1990–1994: An analysis of immigration to New York City in the early 1990s.* New York: Author.

New York City Department of City Planning. (1999). *The newest New Yorkers, 1995–96* (DCP No. 99–08) New York: Author.

Newman, M. (1995, June 1). Giuliani chides Cortines for resisting use of police: School board leader sides with chancellor. *The New York Times,* pp. B3–B4

Noguera, P. (1995). Preventing and producing violence: A critical analysis of responses to school violence. *Harvard Educational Review, 65*(2), 189–210.

Noguera, P. (1999, November 11). Listen first: How student perspectives on violence can be used to create safer schools. *In Motion Magazine* [online]. Retrieved May 21, 2003. Available: http://inmotionmagazine.com/pnlist1. html

Norris, K. (1998). *Amazing grace.* New York: Riverhead Books.

Oakes, J. (1985). *Keeping track: How schools structure inequality.* New Haven, CT: Yale University Press.

O'Connor, S. (1993, May 24). Death in the everyday schoolroom. *The Nation,* pp 702–703.

Olson, C. (1966). *Selected writings.* New York: New Directions.

Ong, W. (1982). *Orality and literacy: The technologizing of the world.* London: Routledge.

Orfield, G. (1995). Housing and the justification of school segregation. *University of Pennsylvania Law Review, 143*(5), 1397–1406.

Orfield, G. (2001, July). Schools more separate: Consequences of a decade of resegregation. The Civil Rights Project, Harvard University [online]. Retrieved February 4, 2004. Available: www.civilrightsproject.harvard.edu/research/deseg/schools_more_separate.pdf

Ostriker, A. S. (1986). *Stealing the language: The emergence of women's poetry in America.* Boston: Beacon Press.

Oxford English Dictionary. (1971). Oxford, UK: Oxford University Press.

Pastor, J., McCormick, J., & Fine, M. (1996). Makin' homes: An urban girl thing. In B. Leadbeater & N. Way (Eds.), *Urban girls: Resisting stereotypes, creating identities* (pp. 15–34). New York: New York University Press.

Patterson, O. (1999, April 30). When they are us. *The New York Times*, p. A31.

Perez-Pena, R. (2002, June 26). Court reverses finance ruling on city schools. *The New York Times*, p. A1.

Perlman, J., & Waldinger, R. (1998, Summer). Are the children of today's immigrants making it? *The Public Interest*, 73–96.

Perry, D. (1997, April-June). Rural ideologies and urban imaginings: Wolof immigrants in New York City. *Africa Today, 4*(2), 229–260.

Pettit, B., & Western, B. (2004, January). *Mass imprisonment and the life course: Race and class inequality in US incarceration.* Paper presented during the Irene Flecknoe Ross Lecture Series, University of California, Los Angeles.

Piccoli, G. (1939, June 27). Letter from Piccoli (head of sculpture division, Federal Arts Project for the City of New York, Works Progress Administration) to Bessie Fielding (secretary, Municipal Art Commission). Municipal Art Commission, City Hall, New York, NY.

At poets' gathering, a tribute to Diallo. (2000, March 27). *The New York Times*, p. B6.

Poulin, A. (1991). *Contemporary American poetry* (5th ed.). New York: Houghton Mifflin.

Preston, J., & Chiles, N. (1990, June 21). Welcome nearly wasn't. *Newsday*, city edition, p. 4.

Probe fire at school in Brooklyn. (1976, March 9). *New York Post*, p. 53.

Rabinow, P. (1984). *Foucault reader.* New York: Pantheon Books.

Raftery, T. (1980, February 13). Prospect High is picketed over safety. *Daily News*, p. K3.

Rich, A. (1993). *What is found there: Notebooks on poetry and politics.* New York: W. W. Norton.

Ricoeur, P. (1974). Violence and language. In S. David & J. Bien (Eds.), *Political and social essays* (pp. 88–101). Athens: Ohio University Press.

Roane, K. (1999, September 14). These grand old schools nurtured a city; some say it is time to tear them down. *The New York Times*, pp. B6, B8.

Rodriguez, R. (1983). *Hunger of memory: The education of Richard Rodriquez.* New York: Bantam Books.

Rose, M. (1995). *Possible lives: The promise of public education in America.* Boston: Houghton Mifflin.

Ross, A. (2002). The odor of publicity. In M. Sorkin & S. Zukin (Eds.), *After the World Trade Center* (pp. 121–130). New York: Routledge.

Rukeyser, M. (1994). The resistances. In J. H. Levi (Ed.), *A Muriel Rukeyser reader* (pp. 120-127). New York: W. W. Norton.

Rushdie, S. (1991). *Imaginary homelands: Essays and criticism 1981–1991.* New York: Penguin Books.

Russakoff, D. (1996, February 13). New York mayor galls GOP by becoming champion of immigrants. *Washington Post*, p. A4.

Sacher, E. (1995, February 15). Danger zone: Indoor play chain enforces tight security at city sites. *New York Newsday*, p. A3.

Scheper-Hughes, N. (1992). *Death without weeping: The violence of everyday life in Brazil.* Berkeley: University of California Press.

Scholes, R. (1998). *The rise and fall of English: Reconstructing English as a discipline.* New Haven, CT and London: Yale University Press.

Schuman, T., & Sclar, E. (1998, March-April). New York: Race, class & space: A historical comparison of the three regional plans for New York. Planners Network. Retrieved September 22, 2003. Available: www.plannersnetwork. org/htm/pub/archives/98.html

Scott, J. (2001a, March 23). The census New York; races still tend to live apart in New York, census shows. *The New York Times*, p. B1.

Scott, J. (2001b, June 18). The census—a region of enclaves; amid a sea of faces, islands of segregation. *The New York Times*, p. A1.

Scott, J. (2001c, July 29). The world adjoining; rethinking segregation beyond black and white. *The New York Times*, sec. 4 (The week in review), p. 1.

Sexton, J. (1994, September 17). As classes resume after a shooting, the subject is safety. *The New York Times*, p. A27.

Snyder, C.B.J. (1908). Public school buildings in the City of New York. *The American Architect and Building News, xciii*(1674), 27–30.

Snyder, C.B.J. (1914). New high school, New York City. *The American Architect and Building News, cv*(2001).

Sontag, D. (1992, November 28). Caribbean pupils' English seems barrier, not bridge. *The New York Times*, pp. A1, A22.

Stanley, A. (1990, June 21). The Mandela visit: Reporter's notebook; pride and confusion mix in a talk on education. *The New York Times*, p. A20.

Steinberg, J. (1992, March 2). Dinkins promises money for safety in violent schools. *The New York Times*, p. A1.

Steinberg, J. (1995, September 7). As high schools open, mayor and Cortines bicker. *The New York Times*, p. B4.

Steinberg, J. (1999, December 3). Academic standards eased as a fear of failure spreads. *The New York Times*, p. A1.

Sterngold, J. (1999, December 2). Los Angeles may ease up on school promotion policy. *The New York Times*, p. A20.

Sullivan, M. L., & Miller, B. (1999). *Adolescent violence, state processes, and the local context of moral panic.* In J. McC. Heyman (Ed.), States and illegal practices (pp. 261–283). Oxford: Berg Publishers.

Tabor, M. (1992, March 4). Slain youth's poem on death is read at Brooklyn funeral. *The New York Times*, p. B3.

Taylor, B. N. (1995, October 14). Cutting class. *The New York Times,* p. A19.

Theoharris, J. F. (1996). *We have to learn to define ourselves, name ourselves and speak for ourselves': Black teenagers, urban schools, writing and the politics of representation.* Unpublished doctoral dissertation, University of Michigan, Ann Arbor.

Torres, A. (1995). *Between melting pot and mosaic: African Americans and Puerto Ricans in the New York political economy.* Philadelphia: Temple University Press.

Toscano, J. (1971, July 10). Lomenzo curbs realty soliciting. *Daily News*, p. 15.

Toy, V. (1995, September 26). Safety plan too little for mayor. *The New York Times,* p. B3.

Tyack, D. (1974). *The one best system: A history of American urban education.* Cambridge, MA: Harvard University Press.

Vergara, C. J. (1994, January 31). The bunkering of the poor. *The Nation*, p. 121.

Vergara, C. J. (1997). The new American ghetto. New Brunswick, NJ: Rutgers University Press.

Waldinger, R., & Lapp. M. (1993, March) Back to the sweatshop or ahead to the informal sector? *International Journal of Urban and Regional Research, 17*(1), 6–29.

Wasserman, J. (1999, September 2). 21,000 get bad news record number left back; social promotion ends. *Daily News*, p. 6.

Waters, M. (1999). *Black identities: West Indian immigrant dreams and American realities.* Cambridge, MA: Harvard University Press.

Weis, L., & Fine, M. (Eds.). (2000). *Construction sites: Excavating race, class, and gender among urban youth.* New York: Teachers College Press.

Wilder, C. S. (2000). *A covenant with color*. New York: Columbia University Press.

Willen, L. (1995, February 1). Truants face cuts. *New York Newsday*, p. A6.

Wilson, W. J. (1996). *When work disappears: The world of the new urban poor*. New York: Alfred A. Knopf.

Young, I. M. (1990). *Justice and the politics of difference*. Princeton, NJ: Princeton University Press.

Index

About the Author

Jennifer McCormick teaches in the Graduate School of Education & Information Studies at the University of California, Los Angeles. Her research interests include the connection between art and literacy, writing in and out of school, and teacher education. Prior to UCLA, she taught at Brooklyn College, where she coordinated Day of the Poet, a community-centered event that brings together high school students from public, parochial, and prep schools in Brooklyn to write poetry and hear nationally known poets. McCormick's articles have appeared in *The Journal of Curriculum Theorizing* and *The Urban Review*.